'Entrepreneurship is a key engine of the modern economy. This book is the essential guide for the founders of the future who want to get started and build the enduring businesses of tomorrow.'

Tony Blair, Executive Chairman of the Institute for Global Change, and former Prime Minister of Great Britain and Northern Ireland

'Alice and Matt have created the ideal handbook for anyone considering founding a company. It provides both strategic advice on building toward a mission and purpose, plus pragmatic advice on the first 100 days. Essential reading for anyone experimenting with ideas and co-founding teams.'

Sara Clemens, former COO, Twitch

'In this book, Alice and Matt explain how they've been helping some of the world's most ambitious and talented people start companies for the last 10 years. It's a great overview of the founding journey.'

Tom Blomfield, founder, Monzo

'Alice and Matt have helped hundreds of founders build companies and this book distils everything they've learned. It's a great starting point for any aspiring entrepreneur!'

Taavet Hinrikus, founder, Wise

T0347589

How to be a Founder

How entrepreneurs
can identify, fund and
launch their best ideas

Alice Bentinck and Matt Clifford

BLOOMSBURY BUSINESS
LONDON · OXFORD · NEW YORK · NEW DELHI · SYDNEY

BLOOMSBURY BUSINESS
Bloomsbury Publishing Plc
50 Bedford Square, London, WC1B 3DP, UK
29 Earlsfort Terrace, Dublin 2, Ireland

BLOOMSBURY, BLOOMSBURY BUSINESS and the Diana logo are trademarks
of Bloomsbury Publishing Plc

First published in Great Britain in hardback 2022
This paperback edition published 2024

A catalogue record for this book is available from the British Library

Library of Congress Cataloguing-in-Publication data has been applied for

ISBN: HB: 978-1-4729-9434-9; TPB: 978-1-3994-1160-8; eBook: 978-1-4729-9432-5

4 6 8 10 9 7 5 3

Typeset by Deanta Global Publishing Services, Chennai, India
Printed and bound in Great Britain by CPI Group (UK) Ltd, Croydon CR0 4YY

To find out more about our authors and books visit www.bloomsbury.com
and sign up for our newsletters

Contents

Foreword   vii

Introduction   I

PART I
The Founder Mindset   9

CHAPTER I
What makes a great founder   II

CHAPTER 2
The myths that stop founders   24

CHAPTER 3
What causes failure and how to avoid it   43

CHAPTER 4
Cultivating the mindset of a founder   51

PART 2
The Founding Process   61

CHAPTER 5
Three and a half rules for ambitious founders   63

CHAPTER 6
Understand your edge   72

CHAPTER 7
How to use your edge   87

CHAPTER 8

Choosing your co-founder 97

CHAPTER 9

Working with your co-founder and testing the team 112

CHAPTER 10

Getting to founder/idea fit 124

CHAPTER 11

Customer Development – finding out your
customer's secrets 139

PART 3

Growing and Scaling 159

CHAPTER 12

An introduction to startup financing 161

CHAPTER 13

How to raise money 175

CHAPTER 14

Preparing for the road ahead 184

CHAPTER 15

Building culture 192

CHAPTER 16

What happens next? 202

Bibliography 207
Acknowledgements 209
Index 211

Foreword

The creation of the future is important. All major institutions today – whether they are companies or countries – had founders. Today's problems will be solved by future companies and future products. Those new institutions will create the future jobs and the infrastructure of society.

Entrepreneurship is a critical part of how we create this future. While existing companies and institutions do provide key innovations, many more innovations are driven by entrepreneurs who see an opportunity for something new. And, as in my personal shorthand, these entrepreneurs jump off a cliff and try to assemble the aeroplane of the new company with its products and services on the way down.

Once you look at the future through this lens – this telescope – you realize how important founders can be. As a society, we need as many founders as possible, and we need to enable these founders to succeed.

In other words, we need to scale entrepreneurship.

Assembling that aeroplane while falling is very difficult, and we need to build the networks that enable these founders to assemble the talent and resources to build the future.

There's a set of in-depth reasons why ongoing innovation and building new, better institutions helps keep our society healthy, happy and productive. Roughly speaking, when people believe that we will have new opportunities, that the future can be substantially better than the past and that there's a chance for more people to win in the future, these are societies that promote healthy collaboration and growth.

Founders building companies is the key part of building these new, better opportunities. In my own career, I've been focused on using networks to create amplifying platforms for entrepreneurship. Whether it's creating an ecosystem for small businesses to build online businesses (PayPal), creating new marketplaces for new kinds of travel businesses (Airbnb) or a pure professional network to help all professionals (LinkedIn) – these are all examples of networks that help amplify entrepreneurs and their businesses.

My friend Toby Coppel of Mosaic Ventures knew about my efforts here, so back in 2016, he encouraged me to meet with Alice and Matt. He told me they were great founders working on an interesting platform called Entrepreneur First who were going to be visiting Silicon Valley, looking to build bridges for their portfolio companies and incubation programs.

I started out as a sceptic. I warned Toby that Silicon Valley is full of failed and irrelevant incubators; that this challenge is very difficult. Usually, incubators create an adverse selection for several good reasons. But Toby has a great eye for talent, so I agreed to meet with them.

Within an hour of meeting Alice and Matt, they had overcome my scepticism and won me over. They were taking a smart shot on goal by innovating on founder selection and geography. Many incubators target only complete teams pitching a specific project already – like a pre-seed or seed investment. Instead, Entrepreneur First focused on bringing the most exceptional people together to build co-founding teams and find the right idea. And rather than limiting itself to people who were already in Silicon Valley, Entrepreneur First was extending its network to founders around the world, from New York to Paris, Bangalore, and of course, London.

All of these cities have a deep reservoir of great technical talent, with plenty of interest in entrepreneurship, but needed an amplifying network to help launch a greater number of capable founders on an entrepreneurial journey because their existing ecosystems were seriously limited in how they support entrepreneurship.

Since that meeting, Greylock Partners and I invested in Alice and Matt, and we've seen them iterate and improve at facilitating the alchemical reaction of bringing together robust co-founders to form compelling businesses. Their OKRs (objectives and key results) focus on providing a better set of services and interactions to catalyse new founding teams.

Of course, even as Entrepreneur First continues to scale, it can't possibly launch even a tiny fraction of the world's aspiring co-founders, which is why I'm so delighted that Alice and Matt have decided to share their secrets with the world in *How To Be A Founder*. I hope this book will help 'blitzscale' entrepreneurship globally.

While *How To Be A Founder* covers the entire entrepreneurial journey, its most groundbreaking idea is its concept of founder 'Edge'. Not only can potential entrepreneurs use this framework to figure out their personal edge, whether it lies in their particular skills (Technical Edge), behaviours (Catalyst Edge) or areas of expertise (Market Edge), but the book also explains how and why founding teams can combine their respective edges to find their 'Founder-Idea Fit'. When co-founders with complementary edges join forces to tackle a problem that requires their specific combination of capabilities, their impact can be amazing.

This gets to one of the subtle but very important parts of both Entrepreneur First and this book. Silicon Valley has been running an intense ecosystem of entrepreneurs creating companies for decades. There are thousands of startups; they compete intensely for everything from talent to capital to customers and revenue. Stunningly, this small geography – which has less than 3.5 million people total, where only a small fraction works in the technology industry – accounts for more than half of the market capitalization on the Nasdaq stock exchange.

Many lessons arise from this intense, fast-moving, competitive, cooperative and inventive ecosystem. Some of these lessons I have put in my own books such as *The Alliance* and *Blitzscaling*. But one key lesson is that founders have a much better success rate when they have co-founders. With a Steve Jobs, you have a Steve Wozniak; with a Bill Gates, you have a Paul Allen.

Today, these dynamic duos are building great companies all around the world, as a new generation of co-founders like Melanie Perkins and Cliff Obrecht in Sydney and Anthony Tan and Tan Hooi Ling in Singapore demonstrate. But the extreme importance of co-founders – both for creating massively scaled companies and for increasing your chances of success – is rarely covered.

Entrepreneur First works intensely to find the best people for their cohorts, giving exceptionally talented people a place to find the right co-founder and rapidly develop a new idea together. This means that Matt and Alice have worked with many hundreds of companies and thousands of entrepreneurs – and one of their unique, key strengths is pushing teams to great outcomes through these frameworks.

Very little has been written about this often-overlooked process of building the co-founder relationship. Matt and Alice have been iterating, learning and improving this process for years. Rather than treating the co-founder relationship like the unknowable mystery of love at first sight, they lay out a counterintuitive but pragmatic approach, including the biggest signal that someone isn't ready to be a founder, the one question you need to ask yourself each day to determine if the team isn't working out and why it's so important to assume that an early breakup is the default outcome, not a personal failing.

There's a phrase deeply associated with Silicon Valley: fail fast. Sometimes people misconstrue this phrase as focused on failure. In fact, it's fail fast so that you spend more effort and time on potential paths to success. Entrepreneur First embodies this lesson in founding team creation.

I highlight this key insight since it's very important, almost unaddressed in all of the startup literature and a significant variable to entrepreneurial success. The book also has other key insights into how to be a founder and how to maximize your chance of success.

Whether you're an aspiring entrepreneur or someone who invests in them, *How To Be A Founder* offers a new and powerful set of lenses for forming and evaluating founding teams.

Reid Hoffman

Introduction

What do you want to be when you grow up?

We all hear this question as children. We probably looked around and saw ourselves as the people we were closest to; we might have seen ourselves as teachers, police officers, engineers, barristers or surgeons. We often form our answers and chart our paths to success around common, visible careers in our community, many of which are noble professions. But if you build your life as an answer to the wrong questions, you miss out on opportunities you never imagined.

The better question might be this: *What are you going to do with your short time on Earth?* If you're thinking in terms of impact, and if you have the desire to reach people beyond your immediate circle, what might be possible? And what is the most powerful tool you need to realize your potential? As Heraclitus said, 'Big results require big ambitions.'

Nothing has shaped human history more than ambition. The power of ambition to spark innovation, fuel progress, and inspire the exploration of new frontiers is the stuff of legends and blockbusters. If there is a problem worth solving, ambition finds a way. How the most ambitious people dedicate their lives has a profound impact on society, the economy and culture.

Across the ages, ambition has always been expressed through the most powerful tools and institutions of the day. What's different today is that *you* have unprecedented access to platforms that allow you to scale your impact to millions, or even billions, of people. The most powerful tool today is entrepreneurship. We believe that being a founder is the ultimate career path for the world's most ambitious people.

If you're reading this book, you likely have the ambition to be an entrepreneur. Lots of people – especially young and ambitious people – say they want to start startups. Very few do. A recent study indicated that 62 per cent[1] of Gen Zs plan to start or have already set up their own business. But if we were to survey a group of students at a leading university today, most would *still* focus their first career choices around traditional roles. We hear it all the time: '*I will be a founder, but let me just do a couple of years at Goldman Sachs or Facebook first.*' When we check up on their progress later, they've become consultants or bankers – and they never leave.

So, why is it that we are in this peculiar situation where lots of talented people want to explore entrepreneurship – and there is an increasingly significant amount of venture capital available to do so – yet so many still hesitate? **Why is the world missing out on some of its best founders?**

A New Kind of Ambition

Our core belief is that starting a technology company today is the most accessible and effective path to having an impact in the world. You can think of career paths as tools for amplifying talent and ambition. Over time, the leverage provided by careers has become more and more powerful. Arguably, it reached a peak with the rise of the modern multinational corporation – if you can rise to the top of one of these, you acquire enormous reach, influence and wealth. That's one reason why big companies – corporations, banks, professional services firms – have become a magnet for talented and ambitious people who want to accelerate a high-impact career.

But there's at least one corner of the world where this default path doesn't hold: Silicon Valley. In the San Francisco Bay Area, the most ambitious people want to build technology companies. And no

[1] Worth. 'What I've Learned from Working with Gen Z Entrepreneurs'. April 16, 2021. https://www.worth.com/gen-z-entrepreneurs/

wonder. Technology entrepreneurship not only offers unprecedented scale – the biggest tech companies reach billions of people *every day* – but as a founder, you have the opportunity to imagine and build the world you want to see, not just take over the controls of a machine someone else has made.

We believe that tech entrepreneurship will become the dominant global ambition in the twenty-first century. If you have what it takes – beginning with ambition – you can build skills to meet the moment and position yourself to achieve incredible impact.

Critique capitalism all you like, but it's better for Elon Musk to tackle everything from electric vehicles to space exploration than to invade a continent. Technology entrepreneurship creates a path for ambition to be a positive, value-creating force for the world. As a founder, your job is to build things that people value, and if you do that at scale, your personal success can create a genuinely positive outcome for humanity.

The Price of Procrastination

There are more opportunities to exercise ambition today than ever before, yet it consistently amazes us how many people say that they don't enjoy their jobs, even though we spend the majority of our waking hours at work.

And yet, too many ambitious people stay on at their jobs. The cumulative impact of delaying your decision increases the longer you stay. One more year in your day job may not feel like it will take you far from the path of becoming a founder, but your lifestyle and goals begin to align very quickly with the position and career path you are in. Instead of exploring entrepreneurial ideas in your free time, you're navigating workplace dynamics and trying to win over your boss.

As it turns out, the real risk isn't starting a company – it's the opportunity cost of delaying your entrepreneurial journey (we'll confront the realities of risk throughout this book). The value you can create as a founder – not just in terms of your personal fortune or fulfilment, but real, world-changing impact – far outstrips the success you could see on any other career path.

There are so many beliefs that fundamentally stop people who could become exceptional founders from ever taking the leap. Our current culture is shaped largely by the media portrayals of entrepreneurs as lone geniuses or buddies-since-nursery-school co-founding duos. Would-be entrepreneurs rule themselves out because they don't want to go it alone or don't have the right co-founder in their existing network. They don't think the timing is right because they've bought into the idea that they're too young and inexperienced or too old and burdened by other responsibilities. They were born in a rural community and not a global city. They don't have the right idea. As we'll demonstrate, none of these need be barriers.

When people talk about the risk of starting a business, they're usually talking about the risk that the financial outcome turns out to be worse than the relative safety of staying in a corporate role. But there's another kind of risk that's rarely discussed that we think is just as important: the risk of never starting up at all, if that's an ambition you think will fulfil you.

When we say, 'The opportunity cost of not starting a company is huge,' we mean that the uncapped upside of a successful entrepreneurial journey – in terms of impact, learning and economics – is so enormous that to miss the boat is potentially tragic. While it's never too late, most people do have a relatively brief window of opportunity in which to explore becoming an entrepreneur. Sacrificing that opportunity by delaying any action could mean passing on your purpose. Not founding the company you were meant to build because there was always a path of less resistance is the biggest opportunity cost of all.

In his essay 'You Weren't Meant to Have a Boss', the venture capitalist Paul Graham compares the lives of programmers working at large corporations to the existence of lions in a zoo: 'I suspect that working for oneself feels better to humans in much the same way that living in the wild must feel better to a wide-ranging predator like a lion. Life in a zoo is easier, but it isn't the life they were designed for.'

The EF Founding Story

Today, our business, Entrepreneur First (EF), is the world's leading investor in entrepreneurial talent. We've helped thousands of people find their co-founders and backed hundreds of companies now worth billions of dollars. But that's not the only reason we're familiar with the barriers to becoming a founder – we experienced them, too. Our own story runs counter to many of the recommendations we've since developed. We did what so many ambitious graduates in the UK seem to do: we set off on a traditional career path as corporate consultants. We'd both thought about being founders in the past, but it was not on our radar as a possible career path in 2008 – especially amidst the uncertainty of the economic crash going on at the time. We didn't know each other as university students but both ended up at McKinsey, largely because it seemed like the kind of employer that would teach us about business without closing any options.

We can attest to the fact that top-tier consultancies are fantastic places for exposure to how different businesses work. But, ultimately, they don't teach you how to be an entrepreneur.

Choosing the consultancy path was also an expression of our ambition. We both knew that McKinsey was incredibly selective. We'd been on that treadmill of collecting badges throughout our lives – doing well in exams, going to prestigious universities – and this felt like the next prize. Once there, we started plotting our futures. After McKinsey, the typical path was to go to business school and get an MBA. But we were both clear that we didn't want that; it seemed to us one more detour from our true path while still avoiding any sort of commitment.

We speak from direct experience. We've been through the early mistakes and formative stages of a startup – mistakes that we hope this book will help you avoid. For instance, we initially got together with three other friends from our cohort, so there were five of us trying to come up with an idea as a group. We built an Excel financial model of the (non-existent) business before we spoke to a single potential customer. We started with a blank sheet of paper and tried to reason from first principles about what a good idea might look like. There wasn't much guidance at the time to help us understand the right way to go about launching a startup. Needless to say, we don't recommend this path.

Eventually, it was just the two of us – Matt and Alice. We're an example of how the strengths and experiences of the team dictate the kind of startup you can create and the scale of the outcome you can have. Because we're both non-technical, it seemed sensible to build a non-technical business. There are downsides to this: it's made scaling our company slower than it's been for some of the software startups in which we've been fortunate to invest. There was huge serendipity in working together – but if you are highly ambitious, and you have a high drive to achieve, you probably don't want to rely solely on serendipity.

We started Entrepreneur First because we came to believe that there were many people like us: ambitious young people with entrepreneurial ambitions who weren't sure how to get started. We turned out to be right, eventually, but as we'll advise later in the book, assuming that there are lots of customers like you isn't always the best starting place for an idea. Although Entrepreneur First has become a global success, many of our challenges in getting started came because we didn't have access to the kind of advice we give founders now. What we realized is that there is so much opacity about the process of starting a company. We didn't even know how to come up with an idea or navigate the world as founders. We learned how to do it by taking other people, eventually thousands of them, through that process. Today, our entire business is about backing individuals at the very start of their entrepreneurial journeys and advising them on how to be founders.

There's a growing body of advice around what to do once you have a team and an idea – how to raise money, how to get to product-market fit. But the part that's still a bit murky is the earliest stage – how to go from being an individual with no team and an un-validated idea to a co-founder of a company. The zero-to-one phase that mystified us in our founding journey is the very phase that we have focused on for the past decade. In this book, we're going to help people understand how you purposefully create what has – until now – been seen as a fortuitous meeting of minds. We are writing this book to demystify what it takes to become an amazing founder. We've walked alongside thousands of people and equipped them with the principles and processes for their journey into entrepreneurship. We've developed accelerator ecosystems in six countries and understand the nuances of geographical and cultural norms. We've seen what it takes and what incredible outcomes are possible by choosing this path.

The thrill of entrepreneurship is being able to imagine a different world and then drag it into reality. Sometimes you might feel like you're dragging it kicking and screaming, but there's such thrill as a founder in seeing new possibilities emerge every day, all over the world.

Your Entrepreneurial Journey

We hope that this book enables you to become a startup founder. We're going to try to give you everything you need to know about being a founder – what to do, when to do it and how to do it – right up until you raise your seed round of funding.

We've split this book into three parts. First, we explore the mindsets and behaviours of people with incredible founder potential. As you read, make note of the criteria you connect with and what you might be missing. We also dispel prevalent myths about founder prerequisites and address the challenges that commonly derail a founder's journey, so you can foresee what might cause you to quit. The second section delves into the Entrepreneur First framework for building your co-founding team and moving through the ideation process. We share numerous examples of how these ideas have shown up in both well-known and emerging companies. Last, we offer advice as you prepare to grow and scale. The book takes you up to the first 'seed' round of funding – the point when you've found traction with customers and are about to take off. Everything we share with you will be based on our decade of experience coaching thousands of startup founders through the process. We've also compiled a few of our most helpful resources at howtobeafounder.com.

PART I

The Founder Mindset

As talent investors, we bet on potential. We look for people who are fuelled by ambition, are motivated by a relentless curiosity, and possess the tenacity to accomplish audacious, world-changing goals. Does this sound like you? In this section, we show how cultivating these attitudes is the critical first step to becoming a founder.

There is no singular profile for founder success, but beginning from a foundation of deep self-knowledge will help you weather the constant challenges (and tastes of success) you will encounter on your entrepreneurship journey. We know this because we've done it ourselves. And we've guided thousands of people just like you through the process of finding a co-founder and launching a successful company. Our goal is to shorten the time frame between when you decide to get started and when your company gets funded. The clock starts now.

CHAPTER 1

What Makes a Great Founder

We know founders. Each year, we evaluate thousands of individuals on their founder potential, and we see first-hand that this path is not for everyone. We look for people who could found high-growth, globally important technology companies – the types of company that would benefit from venture capital funding. We've spent years learning to spot exceptional founders before they've even started a company. Often, the entrepreneurs we work with have never attempted to found before. Some are recent graduates or have little work experience. So how does anyone know if they have what it takes?

While most would-be founders are concerned with whether they know enough, success is not dependent on what you already know. Instead, it's dependent on what you learn through pursuing a particular solution to a particular problem. A relatively small amount of your ability to succeed is what you know how to do on Day One. If it were, then being a venture capitalist would be a much easier job – they could simply suppose success would come for whoever has the most education and experience. Ask any venture capitalist – that's not how it works.

Now, we'll dig more deeply into the abilities, behaviours and mindsets we believe are essential for entrepreneurs based on our years of experience. The collection of characteristics shared here shouldn't be approached as a checklist for success. In our experience, many founders have these seven criteria in common; however it's extremely rare for any individual to possess them all. Look for the ones that resonate with your experience and those that feel like a stretch. Some are innate, but a growth mindset will help you recognize that no characteristic is fixed. We'll offer some questions on how to understand whether you might meet a certain characteristic and examples of those who have.

1. Great founders are outliers.

To understand your trajectory, you need to understand how you stand out from your peers – colleagues, classmates, and other comparable people who've been alongside you at the high points in your career or education. World-class founders are outliers. They are high-potential individuals who have demonstrated exceptional skill and the characteristics needed to win. They think and act differently than those around them. Does this sound like you? Can you think of an outstanding example of something you have achieved, built or created? Is it something that most people around you could not – or would not – have done?

What's important is your ability to succeed *given the opportunities available to you*. Some people think they scored on a breakaway when, in reality, they were set up for a penalty kick with nobody tending goal. There are plenty of examples of founders who are rich white men. However, many, many people who come from more difficult socioeconomic backgrounds, who haven't had access to elite education, or who have experienced barriers due to ethnicity, gender, sexuality or other inequalities have incredible founder potential. They may have had less access to opportunity than others, but *relative to their peer group,* they've set themselves apart. Today, venture capital is, sadly, far from a level playing field. In many ways, it reflects rather than challenges the inequalities of broader society. But it is changing fast, thanks to the efforts of investors who know that entrepreneurial talent is evenly distributed, even if opportunity is not. That's why we care about what you've achieved given the resources you've had. In other words, do you have what it takes to make it big if you give it a shot?

Take someone like Bas de Vries, founder of Limbic, who said of his trajectory, 'I've always really enjoyed making things. I like to find out how things work, and once I do, to improve it in some way or another. By fourteen, I ended up finding out about programming computers and websites, and I was hooked. At sixteen, I launched my first website [a search engine for cars]. During the summer holiday before my last year of high school, I founded Uncover Lab, a tattoo shop for objects [you can still visit this in Amsterdam today]. By the time I turned nineteen, I had built a peer-to-peer payments app, which grew out to be the best rated one in the Netherlands.' Relative to his peer group, Bas achieved an exceptional amount in a very short amount of time.

2. Great founders demonstrate intellectual curiosity.

When it comes to being a founder, we know that smarts matter. This doesn't necessarily mean you've always received top marks. It refers to your ability to process and solve complex problems. And it's not enough to have innate intelligence; it must be intentionally applied and continuously developed.

Founders need to solve both macro problems (How might this market change in the next decade?) and micro problems (How do I design the right incentive package to retain my best employees?). You will be faced with problems you haven't encountered before and will need to quickly assess and resolve them. 'Starting up is very similar to solving puzzles in real life and that is something that I enjoy the most about this journey,' said Flippy co-founder, Srinidhi Moodalagiri.

Demonstrating intellectual curiosity in the face of great challenge is essential. It inspires you to think critically about the industries, markets, technologies and companies with which you have interacted. It helps you overcome obstacles in creative ways. Of course, impressive academic achievements (having studied at a top institution, working with renowned faculty, winning prizes, publishing papers, graduating at the top of your class) are one indicator. But it's equally possible to demonstrate intellectual curiosity having never gone to university.

Maybe you dropped out of school to build something yourself. Perhaps you participate in competitions or engage in hobbies that tax your brain. Or you might be the sort of person who loves to go deep down the rabbit warren of a new topic, following every thread until you've accidentally become an expert.

'What the smartest people do on the weekends is what everyone else will do during the week in ten years. It's a good bet these present-day hobbies will seed future industries,' said Chris Dixon, investor at Andreessen Horowitz. Think about how something like NFTs (Non Fungible Tokens) have gone from a niche interest to the mainstream relatively quickly.

An incredulous inquiry was the starting point for Square's Jack Dorsey. When a friend called him after losing out on an art sale to a potential customer simply because they were unable to accept a credit card payment, Dorsey wondered how he could break down the barriers around such small business transactions. His search for a solution led to the launch of Square, a mobile credit card reader. Innumerable founder stories start with a curious itch that can only be scratched by learning. Dorsey had previously founded Twitter – after dropping out of New York University a semester short of graduating.

3. Great founders demonstrate clarity of thought.

Great clarity of thought is about being able to break down complex problems or ideas until they are simple and easy to understand. The best founders realize that their superpower is seeing simplicity in the complexity surrounding them. This enables them to spot opportunities that others can't, problem solve quickly and communicate to others effectively. This is not about how you speak, although it ultimately presents itself that way.

If you can practise structuring and reframing your ideas and beliefs so that they can be understood by anyone (potential co-founders, customers, employees or investors) you're on the right path. Remember, most conversations about yourself, your company and your technology will be with non-experts. As a founder, you need to be able to explain your work in a way that helps these audiences understand what you're doing and why they should care about it.

Clarity isn't about charisma. It's about how you:

- Turn your beliefs into simple-to-explain opportunities
- Digest and frame large, messy, qualitative data into insight
- Articulate your value to a potential co-founder and identify the opportunities you could work on together
- Express your understanding of an industry and the problems and opportunities within it

In a tech company, it's important to be able to explain deeply technical concepts simply. However great the technology, it will only achieve its potential if non-experts can understand it.

Clarity of thought is a skill that can be cultivated. It can be helpful to write down your ideas in simple structures or practise speaking your ideas out loud. The best founders we have worked with at EF demonstrate clarity of thought when they can explain something that is fiendishly difficult in a couple of sentences. If you ask questions, they can still give simple and clear answers. They have thought deeply about what they're doing and distilled it into what's most important and compelling for that particular listener. As a first step, read up on The Pyramid Principle by Barbara Minto and find more resources at howtobeafounder.com.

4. Great founders articulate how their idea drives a business.
Great founders don't build something simply for the sake of it or because it's fun. A founder's focus should be on customers and real-world problems. This starts with an idea, but it needs to evolve into a business. The co-founding team must demonstrate how this will happen. Founders are charged with proving 'applicability' and must show 'commerciality'.

Applicability refers to the ways your technology can be applied outside of academia or research.

- Can your technology solve real-world problems? Are there opportunities for impact across multiple disciplines?
- Is your technology viable in the real world?

'Commerciality' refers to the business models that you imagine can create and capture value. It's about being market-minded and customer-obsessed.

- Do you get excited thinking about how to both generate value for your customers *and* capture some of that value for your business?
- Can you explain how a product impacts the customer and improves their lives?

Being able to demonstrate applicability and commerciality doesn't require past commercial experience or a sales background. Instead, it's about being market-minded. For example, Rachel Carrell, founder of Koru Kids, knew that there were many obvious problems in childcare but felt 'the secret was that it was possible to create a whole new source of supply of nannies, which no one had done before. I learned that it was possible by just giving it a go. I'd previously worked in healthcare systems, so I thought about childcare as a system as well.' Koru Kids raised their Series A from Atomico, a top European VC.

5. Great founders challenge convention.

Even as entrepreneurship becomes more popular, it's still an unconventional career path for most people. It's unlikely that the first unconventional thing a founder has done is start a company. Most will have been challenging the status quo or making unusual choices throughout their lives. They might have made high-risk choices (such as turning down a stable job to pursue something interesting) or taken a non-linear path in life, bouncing between seemingly disconnected areas of interest. Great founders often intentionally put themselves in uncomfortable situations to grow or achieve something. Usually, that means doing work that might be completely outside of their comfort zone or having side projects that are about building something without a blueprint.

The founders of Lottie Lab, Andrew Ologunebi and Alistair Thomson, were both used to challenging convention from a young age. Andrew built a ten-person design consultancy team that worked with major global brands during his undergraduate degree. Alistair built a game as a child that, by the time he was eighteen years old, had been played millions of times.

Sasha Haco, CEO and co-founder of Unitary, was used to excelling academically – having been top of her year in natural sciences at the University of Cambridge and then doing her PhD supporting one of the world's most famous physicists, Stephen Hawking. The path set out for her was in academia. But she turned down a highly competitive postdoc at Harvard in favour of becoming a founder.

One thing that conventionally successful people find hard about starting a company is that there's no mark scheme to ace or career ladder to climb. Many smart, ambitious people succeed in life by learning how to make their boss look good. That's a real skill, but it won't help you much as a founder. We found this difficult ourselves when we were getting started. Being a startup founder is a praise-free zone. Both the joy and the pain of entrepreneurship is learning to substitute objective metrics – How many customers do you have? How much are they paying you? – for what other people think about how you're doing.

This is why it's helpful to have previous experience carving a path outside a conventional structure or institution. Not only does it cultivate a mindset that will make you more resilient as you build your business, but it teaches you how to get things done when there's no instruction manual.

Think about ways you have challenged convention in the past:

- When did you go out of your way to build or learn something or put yourself on an unusual path?
- What have you done that's seemed odd or counterintuitive to most people?
- What unusual or surprising beliefs or hobbies do you have?
- What do your friends find weird about you?
- What are you obsessive about? And what have you done to cultivate this obsession?
- How have you challenged rules or got around barriers or social norms in order to make something happen?

Ben Silbermann, CEO and co-founder of Pinterest, intended to become a doctor like his ophthalmologist parents and two older sisters. As a high school student in Iowa, Silbermann participated in the prestigious Research Science Institute at MIT. He enrolled in pre-med at Yale before changing course, majoring in political science, and graduating in 2003.

Silbermann started his career as a consultant but eventually set his sights on Silicon Valley where he landed a job in Google customer support. 'It felt like this was the story of my time,' he told Fortune in 2012, 'and I just wanted to be close to it.'[2] But as a non-engineer, Silbermann felt his ability to develop products and make an impact was capped, so he quit to explore entrepreneurship. His first attempt, a shopping app called Tote, failed. The idea for Pinterest was born out of his love of creating collections as a kid. Even though the path challenged convention, much of the early traction for the company (which raised $1.43 billion in its IPO [initial public offering] in 2019) came from his hometown connections. One of its most popular pinners, with millions of followers, is a woman named Jane Wang – Silbermann's mother.

[2] Fortune. 'Is Pinterest the next Facebook?' March 22, 2012. https://fortune.com/2012/03/22/is-pinterest-the-next-facebook/

6. Great founders are fuelled by a drive to achieve.

Building a startup is an uphill race on a poorly marked course that, in the beginning, has very few spectators. For a long time, no one is watching to see how hard you push. That's why possessing an internal drive to do more – a record of striving to achieve – is key. You must have a bias to action and a drive to build, create and grow. How competitive are you? How willing are you to work hard and push forward when there's no clear or determined prize? Think of a time when you've run through walls to make things happen.

Great founders strive to excel – not just in intellectual pursuits, but in sports, hobbies, competitive gaming, side projects, etc. Demonstrating drive to achieve means you've pushed through something difficult or unpleasant to accomplish a goal. You've persisted through significant barriers and achieved something against all odds. And importantly, would you have done it if you thought no one was watching? Are you innately motivated, or are you looking for praise and badges from others?

Melanie Perkins, CEO and co-founder of the online design platform Canva, dropped out of university at nineteen to pursue her first startup, Fusion Books. That drag-and-drop software for designing student yearbooks became the inspiration for her current business, which transformed the design industry and made Perkins one of the wealthiest women in the world. (A funding round reported at the time of this writing valued Canva at $40 billion. Perkins and her co-founder-turned-spouse Cliff Obrecht owned at least 30 per cent of the company at that time, as disclosed in a post on Medium.[3])

Perkins demonstrated her drive to achieve and entrepreneurial tendencies as a teenager. During high school, she routinely woke up at 4.30 a.m. to train as a figure skater. The enterprising Australian started her first business as a teen, selling handmade scarves at shops and markets in Perth.

---

[3] Bloomberg. 'Husband–Wife Team Worth $12 Billion After Latest Canva Funding Round'. September 23, 2021. https://www.bloomberg.com/news/articles/2021-09-23/how-a-husband -wife-team-built-a-12-billion-fortune-with-startup-canva

Drive to achieve often expresses itself as ambition. Many founders describe a feeling of knowing that they could – or even that they were 'meant to' – achieve something big, important or extraordinary. This can backfire, of course; hubris is behind some of the most famous startup failures. But if you're going to go down the path of building a venture-backed business, the belief that you can, or even must, build something big is necessary – even if it's not sufficient.

7. Great founders can create followership.
To build a startup, you need to be able to get other people on board with your vision – whether that's investors, talent, customers or potential co-founders. You'll need to get them excited about your mission and inspire them to help you bring your ideas to life. Have you been able to motivate others to follow your decisions and actions in the past?

It's easy to call yourself a leader. The proof is in whether others choose to follow you. Creating followership requires a blend of leadership skills and persuasive influence. We aren't talking about growing a social media fan base – although once you have a product, that could be helpful. Have you ever led a team of any type? What are your experiences with trying to bring people together and get them behind a common goal? Have you ever worked to convince someone more senior than you to work on a project or go along with an idea? This can express itself in many different ways, especially early in your career. For example, we've funded many people whose experience of leadership is running events, organizing campaigns or leading sports teams.

Alice Pelton, founder of The Lowdown – a contraception review site – persuaded Instagram influencers and celebrities to endorse the site. 'I worked at a big media company, and I had access to the "guests for the day" list. Whenever someone interesting or relevant came into the building (to meet with journalists or go on radio, for example), I would make sure I was in the area, I would say hello and tell them about The Lowdown. It worked really well and got us some great early endorsers.'

These seven areas should give you an idea of whether you have the profile and traits that we have seen successful founders exhibit time and time again. To summarize, exceptional founders are typically on an accelerated life path before they even start a company. They are great problem solvers who can structure complex thoughts to generate insight. They have an innate drive to make things happen and have done this many times outside the status quo. And finally, they know that being a founder is not a loner's journey – it's about taking other exceptional people with you to manifest your vision.

'The word "exceptional" gets thrown around a lot,' said Zoe Jervier Hewitt, who leads talent for Sequoia Capital in Europe. 'We want to find the exceptional people because they are exceptions – to rules, to environments, to groups. They might think of themselves as hireable, but to be honest, they may not work in conventional jobs because you need that well-rounded personality. Exceptional people are probably quite spiky characters, and for entrepreneurship, you don't need to be well-rounded.'

Exceptional individuals with 'spiky' profiles can often represent neurodiversity. Neurodivergent people might possess a less-typical cognitive variation, such as autism, dyslexia or attention deficit hyperactivity disorder (ADHD). Often categorized as a disability, these different ways of processing information can be a superpower for problem-solving and creative thinking – and they're more common than you might think. One in ten people in the UK is neurodivergent.[4] Neurodiversity can be an asset for entrepreneurship.

Mogul Sir Richard Branson and IKEA founder Ingvar Kamprad have both shared publicly about their ADHD diagnosis. Researcher Johan Wiklund – Al Berg Chair and Professor of Entrepreneurship at Syracuse

---

[4] Exceptional Individuals. 'Neurodiversity & Neurodivergent: Types & Meanings'. Accessed November 19, 2021. https://exceptionalindividuals.com/neurodiversity/

University's Whitman School of Management – found that the ability to achieve a state of hyperfocus on certain tasks, when paired with a 'logic of impulsivity' that allows them to respond quickly in high-risk situations, can give entrepreneurs with ADHD an advantage.

While we believe that great founders are everywhere, we need to be clear: founding is not for everyone. There is no fail-proof formula for creating a startup. There is no perfect mould for a successful startup founder. It's not a paint-by-numbers experience. It's not the path to fulfil a fantasy of 'being your own boss' or because you couldn't find a more traditional job.

Being a founder is one of the most demanding ways you could spend your time. There's nothing wrong with wanting to start a *4-Hour Workweek*-inspired lifestyle business, but that's not what this book is about. This book is for people who want to found a venture-backed, high-growth startup that could one day be a public company. If you aren't ready, willing and able to commit the majority of your waking hours to obsessing over your idea, this probably isn't the right path for you.

We know it can look glamorous, but that's not the day-to-day reality. The reason startup workspaces are known for having ping-pong tables and beer onsite is not because they're intrinsically fun, but because most teams have little time to leave the building. When you consider whether to become a founder, you need to understand the potential cost to your private life. It's perfectly possible to combine building a high-growth company with a fulfilling relationship and a happy family life – we both do – but anyone who tells you that there are no trade-offs or that you can do it all with 35-hour weeks is probably kidding you.

Most of the world's wealthiest people are founders, but this is not the best path to getting rich – at least not quickly. If you compare the average long-term income of founders and employees, employees do better. You should only choose to be a founder if you think you're going to be a lot better than average.

Although we think that anyone who has the right characteristics should go for it, we don't think that just anyone can do it. The more we think of founding as a high-skill, high-demand professional vocation, the more likely we are to see people who will ultimately benefit from the journey of becoming entrepreneurs.

Chapter Summary

Although there is no singular profile for founder success, there are common characteristics that many successful founders share.

- Great founders have often gone against the grain, even before they found their first startup. They are comfortable challenging convention and forging different paths from their peers.
- Great founders can communicate through complexity to articulate their ideas and win followers in the process.
- Great founders have an innate drive to achieve. They are often deeply curious and competitive.

CHAPTER 2

The Myths that Stop Founders

In the words of Voltaire, '*Il meglio è l'inimico del bene*' – the best is the enemy of the good. We meet a lot of potential founders who think they can't become a founder because they don't have a perfect idea, a lot of experience or a network. As it turns out, these are not prerequisites.

The idea of 'readiness' is a misunderstanding of what it is actually like to start a company. You discover whether you are cut out to start a particular company through the act of starting it. There is the old adage that you can't become an exceptional pianist by just reading books; you have to spend hours at the piano. The same is true of being a founder. The best way to prepare yourself to become a globally impactful founder is to start a company and learn by doing. It's impossible to know everything you would need to know on Day One. Until you start to scale, most of your time is spent doing things that you don't know how to do. In fact, you're often trying things that *no one* knows how to do. It requires a leap of faith because you're solving for the unknown and figuring out what customers want. Founders must live and work within imperfection as part of the job. Enjoying the chaos and the creativity that the chaos enables is a key part of your role. Chasing perfection in any stage of your startup is a fool's errand, especially when you are in the process of developing an idea.

In this chapter, we outline each of the myths that keep people from starting a company. We've seen these myths stop some of the most ambitious and talented people. Knowledge is power – once you know the reality, myths won't hold you back.

Myth 1: I don't have the right badges

You are super-smart. You're highly competitive. You've always been on top of everything you've done – including building impressive side projects in your free time. You want proof that you are as good as you know you are – a place at a prestigious university, a master's degree, a top-tier job, one more promotion – before you leap into becoming a founder. Partly, you think you'll be 'ready' to be a founder later in life. You believe that the credential is a worthwhile hedge against potential failure. It's easy for ambitious people to get sucked into the trap of 'credentialism' or the culturally approved game of 'badge collecting'. In many cases, this same drive for success results in delaying – and in many cases, extinguishing – entrepreneurial aspirations. Often, you'll have a choice – implicitly or explicitly – between starting a company and gaining another credential. The danger comes not because credentials are bad in themselves (we are grateful for fully credentialed medical professionals, for example), but because they don't translate into entrepreneurial success.

Credentialism presents four problems for aspiring founders: it encourages you to think about 'readiness' to start a company in the wrong way; it trains you to think progress is equivalent to winning approval from a third party, like your boss; it teaches you to adopt a set of values that are rooted in the status quo (rather than seeking to change it); and it conditions you to avoid risk. Let us make something clear: you'll never feel entirely ready. You will learn by doing.

This false mindset isn't entirely your fault – cultural norms play a huge role. Many of us feel the pressure of our families, peers, professors or partners to make the socially approved career move. We crave external validation and want to land a coveted position that makes everyone proud. Preferably one that comes with a sizable pay cheque to pay for the trappings of success and a pension that provides a sense of security. This path makes it easy for your parents to boast to the neighbours, and it feels like the natural progression from your high-achieving youth. You tell yourself you'll scratch that entrepreneurial itch later – after you've gained some experience and established some credibility. You believe that will make you more successful as an entrepreneur.

Most people want to believe the pathway looks like this: earn the badge, ride the prestige, build the network, secure the money, come up with the idea and hook the co-founder. This is a false belief. More time in the workforce or another advanced degree does not necessarily make you a better entrepreneur. It's striking how many of the truly great founders had very little experience outside their own company (in Chapter 6 on understanding your Edge, we'll talk about what sufficient experience looks like). Partly, this is because so much of founding a great company is in ignoring (or at least questioning) well-established standards. By focusing on the pursuit of credentials and badges, you're more likely to become attached to the corporate mindset and way of life – and never start that entrepreneurial endeavour at all. You lock yourself into golden handcuffs.

We often think of a friend who rose to become a partner in a professional services firm. We were talking about entrepreneurship over coffee. 'You know, I would have loved to have started a company, but obviously it's too late for me,' he said. 'I just couldn't take the salary hit.'

He was only thirty years old when he said this! The challenge was that he was already making great money. He was simply unwilling, or unable, to adjust his consumption to the uncertain income of an entrepreneur.

It's not just about age. And it's not just a tension people in elite positions must navigate. You accumulate obligations (mortgages, student loans, children) and expectations (expensive holidays, a taste for luxury), so the immediate hit to the life you've built is too disruptive to take the plunge.

We're not suggesting that anyone over thirty who has a home and kids can't start a company. The academic literature suggests that, on average, older founders are *more* successful. But think about why that might be. For most people, the window of time in which you can duck out of the race to collect prestige badges, go down to a very low salary for six months or more and tolerate unpredictability is very narrow. If you're an experienced and well-established professional, and you're *still* willing to quit your job, that suggests you have a very high conviction that the idea you're pursuing is an exceptionally good one. But that's a very high bar – one that most people will never be able to clear while also working a full-time job. If you look at the history of great companies, you see that many were started from a place of exploration, not immediate conviction. So, if you think right now *might* be a good time, don't kid yourself that the window will be open for ever.

Remember, it's dangerous to reason from a handful of outliers. Yes, Bill Gates and Mark Zuckerberg founded what became trillion-dollar companies as teenage college dropouts, but that doesn't mean every nineteen-year-old with an idea should quit school. Equally, though, averages are likely to be misleading. The average startup fails! If you plan to have the average outcome, it's better not to start at all. What we can say though, both from our own experience and from the broader market, is that exceptional individuals can succeed at any age. The CEOs of Entrepreneur First's five most valuable companies all had a year of work experience or less when they joined us. Don't let badges be the barrier.

Breaking down the barrier:
On some level, we all care about what our peers will think – validation seeking has been a sensible strategy for much of humanity's existence. Today, this is often true for our careers, particularly if you are a highly motivated and ambitious individual. So much of our identity is built around our jobs that the thought of leaving prompts an existential crisis. After all, '*What do you do?*' is often the first question when you meet new people. It's shorthand for asking who you are. If you get to the point where people are

impressed by your answer because your career has a lot of cachet, you'll have to ask yourself if you are willing to reinvent yourself and let that go.

We coach people who are still on the fence about entrepreneurship by encouraging them to stack rank their priorities. If you can identify where you are seeking validation as a primary motivation, you can make progress by acknowledging this, reflecting on why this is true for you, and working out what it will take to move on. It can be useful to closely examine what decisions you have made in the past and what was the real motivating factor behind them. People often don't like what they see when they are honest with themselves. What we say is important to us can be quite different to how we behave – acknowledging this and exploring it is the first step to making change.

Examine that list and assess how your decisions are truly driven. Many people will make the list and acknowledge they don't like the motivating factors but feel they're inescapable. Others do this exercise and seize control. They choose to reject artificial barriers such as peer approval, badge collecting, or perceived status and money.

If you're setting out to create something totally new, you will always run the risk of looking foolish. Founders must be willing to let go of what others think.

Myth 2: I don't have a big enough network

Having a great network in your industry can be an advantage when you know exactly what you're building and selling. Networks can be a shortcut to distribution. But startups are rarely in this position at the beginning; they're still refining their understanding of the problem and figuring out the right solution – distribution is a problem for later. In this case, having a big network in the market you're going after can be a double-edged sword. We worked with a founder who had a decade of experience in finance, and he wanted to build a fintech startup.

He knew the people, he (thought he) knew the product he wanted to build, and he knew who he had to sell it to.

Two problems: first, a bigger network sometimes means greater fear of public failure. This founder didn't want to engage his close contacts to test the early idea. He was worried it wasn't good enough and didn't want to embarrass himself by showing something half-baked to big-name people in his industry. He'd spent a decade as a leader within his market and didn't want to risk that hard-earned reputation. So, he underused his network and didn't learn quickly enough. It turned out to be a disadvantage rather than an advantage.

The second: when you do use your network, it can give you a misleading signal. Most people are conflict-averse. If you're asking your close contacts about an idea as a method of customer development, they will often try to support you by giving the people-pleasing answer rather than the useful answer. When this founder finally asked his customers what they wanted, he needed to hear criticism. Instead, he heard that it sounded like a good idea from well-meaning connections and friends. You want your prospective customers to give you criticism. It's better to hear, 'Terrible idea. I am never gonna buy this,' right out the gate than polite praise.

As a founder, you will ultimately need to build a broad and deep network, but the way to go about it might not be what you imagine. The network that you're initially looking to develop is within the particular *customer group* you're going after – and in the end, in many or even most markets, the best product wins.[5] You build the network you need by having something to offer, not by going back a long way with insiders. As we'll discuss when we talk about generating ideas, you want to be working in a space where you can bring something special to the table.

---

[5] There are some exceptions where a bad product with good distribution can win for a long time or even indefinitely. If you want to enter one of these markets, you probably *do* need a great network on Day One and this advice wouldn't apply.

Some potential founders worry that they don't know any investors. This is understandable, as access to capital is usually an important ingredient of startup success. But, while there's still lots of room for improvement, venture capital is much more open than it used to be. We'll talk about fundraising in more detail later, but the good news is that many organizations exist – such as accelerators like Y Combinator and talent investors like Entrepreneur First – that specialize in funding companies and individuals who *aren't* already plugged into the startup ecosystem. You don't need an introduction or referral to get in; you apply through a simple online form.

The other thing to remember is there's no concept of 'paying your dues' in startups. Because so many of the breakout startup success stories are of people who weren't 'qualified' on paper to build what they did, taking a chance on unproven talent is a core value of most startup ecosystems. Even if you are an unknown, if you have an interesting story or exceptional background, many people will want to talk to you. That's as true when you're twenty-two as it is when you're forty-two, although your approach might look different at various career stages. If you're early in your career, you benefit from your green-ness. Many professionals want to give young people the benefit of the doubt and offer them a leg up. Successful people often want to 'pay it forward', and it's compelling to be part of someone's story from the start. Peter Thiel, billionaire entrepreneur and venture capitalist, famously made more money giving teenage dropout Mark Zuckerberg his first cheque than he did founding PayPal.

Of course, no one will simply open a door for you because of your youth or your experience. You still have to hustle and be prepared for a lot of rejection. It takes real effort, but wherever you are on the experience continuum, there are ways that you can make the stage you're in right now work for you. One huge benefit for aspiring founders today is that so many of the leading figures of startups and venture capital have active social media profiles or public email addresses. Yes, they're likely inundated with inbound messages, but many will respond to a well-crafted cold email. We outline the practice in Chapter 11, Customer Development. Today, no network is no excuse.

Myth 3: I don't live in Silicon Valley

There's a reason Silicon Valley is the startup capital of the world. It's not something in the water; it's about cultural expectation. Had they come of age in the UK, Google co-founders Larry Page and Sergey Brin might have ended up working in a hedge fund. In Singapore, perhaps they'd have become high-flying civil servants. Most ambitious people end up taking the culturally accepted path for 'people like them'. But because Larry and Sergey were based in Silicon Valley, starting a company was a natural step for them – even as academics. In fact, one of their first investors was one of their professors at Stanford. There was an ecosystem of advice, capital and belief to support them from Day One.

We are often asked why Europe doesn't have a Google equivalent. Why is it that locations outside of Silicon Valley have struggled to produce behemoth companies at the same rate? Ecosystem expectations are a huge factor. Founders want to be where it's easy to find fellow risk-takers. An agglomeration of funding, mentorship and startup-friendly professional services is an incredible asset. Plugging into dense networks of people who understand the idiosyncrasies of building a high-growth company from scratch has a compounding effect.

To be successful, you will be dependent on people who understand what you are doing – people who are willing to bet on you throughout your journey. You need investors who will assume significant risk before you have real revenue. You need team members willing to trade the benefits of traditional careers for the equity they could earn working on your product. You need customers who are willing to buy from a company that might not be there next year and suppliers willing to do business with an entity that might disappear. You need skilled service professionals such as lawyers and accountants who understand the weirdness of startup companies relative to more established businesses. Because of those needs, the value of startup ecosystems is enormous. As our friend and investor Reid Hoffman likes to say, it's the network density of Silicon Valley that explains its extraordinary success.

But the odds are, you *aren't* reading this book while seated at the Starbucks on Sand Hill Road, conveniently located between Stanford University and several large VC firms. The good news is that geography is much less of a limiting factor for potential founders than it was in the 1990s for three big reasons.

First, the internet has allowed startup knowledge to spread around the world. The advice that used to be concentrated in the heads of a small number of founders and investors within a ten-mile radius of Palo Alto is now accessible on the web. Organizations like First Round Capital have done an outstanding job of curating the very best advice, which is a boon for founders everywhere.

Second, partly fuelled by internet accessibility, large and thriving ecosystems have emerged thousands of miles from the San Francisco Bay Area. These ecosystems are increasingly anchored by breakout success stories that even ten years ago we might have thought unlikely outside Silicon Valley. From Spotify (Sweden) to Darktrace (the UK), Grab (Singapore) to Flipkart (India), it's clear that it's now possible to build companies worth tens of billions of dollars all over the world.

Third, Silicon Valley itself has become more outward-looking. The joke used to be that if a Bay Area VC couldn't hail a cab to a startup's HQ, they weren't interested in investing. That's changed beyond all recognition. As of this writing, VC funding to startups in Europe went from $18.5 billion for the first half of 2020 to $59 billion in the first half of 2021.[6] In Southeast Asia, startups raised over $8.2 billion in 2020, which was a huge improvement from years prior. But in the first half of 2021, they raised $124.8 billion – an 83 per cent increase from the year before.[7]

The coronavirus pandemic dramatically accelerated a trend that was already evident. The best investors want to invest in the best founders, wherever they are – even if they can't meet in person. So, if you have an internet connection and a high-potential company, it matters less and less where you are physically.

That's not to say that Silicon Valley is over. If you want to build a global technology company, part of the path to scale should still run through Silicon Valley. Particularly, once you reach the point of hundreds of employees and tens of millions in revenue, you're likely to find that many of the customers and much of the executive talent you need is in California. But that does not necessarily mean that you need to have your HQ there, and it certainly doesn't mean that you have to start the company there. Increasingly, Silicon Valley is a way of thinking and working, not a physical location.

Breaking down the barrier:
Imbibing the mindset, norms and values of high-growth startups is important, but it's not location-dependent. You can be in Bangalore, London, Singapore or Des Moines – wherever there's broadband. There are some advantages to founding outside of the Valley, too. Northern California is now one of the most expensive places in the world. But access to Silicon Valley advisors, investors, knowledge, best practice and aspirations is now almost anywhere you want to be. That's why we see record-breaking amounts of capital from

---

[6] Teare, Gené. 'European Startups Got A Bigger Share Of Record Global VC Invested In H1 2021'. Crunchbase News, July 15, 2021. https://news.crunchbase.com/news/european-vc -funding-h1-2021/.
[7] TechCrunch. 'Investors Are Doubling down on Southeast Asia's Digital Economy'. Accessed September 30, 2021. https://social.techcrunch.com/2021/09/09/investors-are-doubling-down -on-southeast-asias-digital-economy/.

Silicon Valley flowing into other startup ecosystems. The eyes of the world are now on places that would have seemed unlikely hubs ten years ago, and the biggest names in tech are taking a global perspective today. That means opportunity for the individual. Just as you no longer need to see geography as a constraint to your ambition, technology opens up vast networks of potential co-founders and teams you can work with on your idea. Remote and global collaboration is like fuel to the fire in emerging hubs such as Mexico City, Buenos Aires, Nairobi and Lagos. This heralds a future where *many* more of the world's most ambitious people can and will choose to become founders.

Myth 4: I can't start because I might fail

Failure is, alas, a fact of startup life. However much experience you have, however good your idea might be, however much capital you raise, you can still fail. Indeed, *most* startups fail. You absolutely *can* reduce the risk – in fact, the whole of the next chapter is about the causes of failure and how to avoid them – but you can't eliminate it. It's not surprising that when we talk to people who say becoming a founder is important to them but say now isn't a good time, there's usually an underlying anxiety: *Do I want to go into an endeavour where the chances of failure are so high?*

That's a valid concern. And there's an obvious critique of investors like us who encourage people to start companies: we have a diversified portfolio and benefit if any of them succeed, whereas a founder is all-in on their (one) company. We believe that today, the proposition for founders has never been so asymmetric – enormous upside if things work, and limited downside if they don't.

What a lot of people don't understand is that the risk in startups is front-loaded. You're most likely to fail at the beginning – but at the beginning, you've lost very little if things don't work out. One sensible model is to give yourself six months to start a company. If it fails, you've lost six months. Most of us can afford to lose that time; it's barely more than a sabbatical. Even if things don't work out, there's value in finding out as early as possible where your skills and interests lie as a founder. If you have the potential to found a globally important company, but you don't try, that is the opportunity cost you should be most worried about.

There undoubtedly was a period when failing as an early-stage founder had negative consequences – but that era is long gone. We've heard lots of potential founders worry that if they fail, they'll have a black mark on their CV and henceforth be unemployable. Today, if anything, the opposite is true. The expansion of a global ecosystem of people who've made a career in and around startups means increased appreciation for the value of trying and failing and the lessons learned in building a business. That attitude spreads. Investors love to back second-time entrepreneurs – being a founder is a skill that you can get better at with repeated attempts – and other startups often want to hire founders whose companies didn't work out. As innovation continues to grow in importance in the broader economy, even big companies are recognizing the value of hiring out-of-box thinkers. Entrepreneurial action is seen as evidence of the drive to achieve, willingness to challenge the status quo and ability to get things done. Today, being a 'failed founder' (while not something we'd encourage you to aim for!) is more likely to be a badge of honour than a bad sign.

We also think it's easy to underestimate the costs of a traditional career for ambitious people. It's true that a traditional career is an effective mechanism to reduce risk of a loss of income or a salary drop. Most careers have relatively clear progression paths. The requirements for moving to the next stage are often transparent, and the success factors required are equally obvious. If you're the sort of person who likes linear progress, there's a lot to appreciate about traditional careers.

However, if you are an ambitious person – and like many founders, an impatient one – traditional career paths can be limiting. They're hard to accelerate, and it's tricky to circumvent the progression of roles and teams created by the organization you work within. Typically, you will have to climb metaphorical ladders and jump hoops to make it into the C-suite. Even if you feel that you should be able to level up more quickly, the constraint may have nothing to do with your ability or even your output but the structure and politics of the organization. Even once (if!) you do make it to the top, the potential for growth is often capped by the scale and history of the institution.

One of the best things about being an entrepreneur is that, in exchange for additional work-life risk (such as lack of clarity about progression and what it's actually going to take to succeed), you have the potential for uncapped upside. That's true at a financial level, of course, but it's also true for intellectual stimulation, for personal and professional growth, for pursuing your interests, for being able to focus on what you're good at, and for designing roles and problems to work on that are most fulfilling. All these dimensions are uncapped when you start a company – as long as you start the right company for you.

We often live life as though we're trying to maximize next year's salary, particularly in structured careers. If I make my boss look good this year, I'll get a bonus or a promotion. That's true, and the predictability of regular pay rises is valuable, but at the end of people's lives, they very rarely add up the sum of their salary to evaluate their life. What did you do that was meaningful? What do you regret never taking the chance to do?

Breaking down the barrier:
When Jeff Bezos was considering whether to leave his (lucrative) corporate job to create an internet-based bookstore, he used a mental model he called a 'Regret Minimization Framework' to explore the question. It's simple: project yourself into the future and ask: 'In X years, will I regret not doing this?'

When you take a holistic life view to weigh an important decision, you're able to focus on what ultimately matters. Regret usually comes from failing to try, not what you tried that didn't work. That's why 'now' is so often the best time. The downside is limited. Companies can fail, but the founders don't have to go down with the ship. We like to say that the company-level risk as a founder is always high, but the career-level risk is not. And, as we'll discuss in the next chapter, there's a lot you can do to reduce the risks. The Regret Minimization Framework prompts you to think about your career as a way to build the life you want to live. Rather than focusing on short-term optimization around incremental raises, you pursue the dream. If it doesn't work out, at least you won't have to live wondering 'what if?'

With the last two myths, you won't find sections titled 'Breaking down the barrier'. We have written entire chapters to answer these particular myths because diversity of founders and their backgrounds and experiences, and the process of working with an idea, are integral parts of the process we're going to teach you. But it's still important to dispel some of the false thinking around these two myths before we get started in Part 2.

Myth 5: I don't fit the 'founder stereotype'

There is no reason why any demographic should be inherently better at founding. We believe there are world-class examples of founders from every type of background. However, as we touched on in the previous chapter, if you make a list of the globally recognizable names in entrepreneurship, you might think that to be a successful founder, you need to be a wealthy, young, white male. We cannot dismiss the role privilege plays in advantage as a founder. When you look at who starts startups, there is a big bias towards white men. Further, a disproportionate number of the people we encounter in our entrepreneurial ecosystems went to private schools (although the percentage is markedly lower than what we saw in consulting). Current norms are heavily skewed, largely because of the privilege of wealth. Clearly, access to finance is harder if you have no money to begin with. But that's starting to change.

Technological advances are democratizing entrepreneurship. Costs of starting a company have decreased sharply. You can now rent assets like web servers for a few dollars, which, in the past, you would have had to spend millions to acquire. And, as we'll discuss in our chapter on fundraising, there are many more ways to access the first cheque. The idea of the 'friends and family' financing round always pointed to the degree of privilege embedded in the entrepreneurial ecosystem, but – fortunately – it's no longer an essential or even common starting point for capital. As we argued earlier, entrepreneurial ecosystems have a strong incentive to treat you based on what you might become, not what you are today. Attitudes about what high potential founders look like are changing. There are still inclusion and diversity issues in venture capital, but it's striking how quickly funds and investors are moving to fill the gap. This is happening partly because they think it's the right thing to do and partly because it's an amazing financial opportunity to fund great founders who might otherwise be overlooked. With increased awareness and incentives, ecosystems evolve.

The shift we see in the way investors are seeking out and putting money behind founders from underrepresented groups is backed up by research. First Round Capital, one of the world's leading VC firms, did a review of their first decade of investments and discovered female-founded companies significantly outperformed male co-founding teams. Their research also points to the power of diverse teams for long-term value creation. As we see more and more proof around the positive financial outcomes of investing in diversity, the money coming in will only grow. We've also seen that diversity and inclusion are increasingly high on the agenda of limited partners – the institutional capital allocators who provide cash for VCs to invest and are effectively the gatekeepers for new investors seeking to raise funds. Like everyone else, VCs respond to incentives.

The reasons women and people of colour are currently less represented among successful founders begin long before making the choice to pursue a particular career path. In school and the media, girls and young women are often told – implicitly or explicitly – that a career in startups or technology isn't for them. Thankfully, some ambitious NGOs and equity-minded accelerators – such as Chloe Capital, Uncharted and Propeller – are working to address this. Sexism and racial bias have also impacted those who had access to opportunities, just as they have in the corporate sphere. For that reason, it's important that when founders from less represented backgrounds look at the statistics on representation in tech, they don't see it as evidence of the future but as a snapshot of data from the past.

There's still a long way to go, but the direction of travel is positive – and the flywheel is starting to turn faster and faster. Role models matter, and there are more and more prominent unicorn founders from underrepresented groups, such as Katrina Lake of Stitch Fix or Oliver Kent-Braham of Marshmallow. We also see, in every geography in which we operate, an enormous desire from founders to give back as mentors, advisors and investors to the next generation. We don't want to underplay the challenges, but there's never been a better time to start a company as someone from an underrepresented group.

Myth 6: I have to have the perfect idea

We hear this all the time: would-be entrepreneurs say they'll quit their job when they have the perfect idea. People tend to make this mistake because they're thinking about what an idea *is* in the wrong way. If ideas existed as pre-packaged things that you could just pluck off the shelf fully formed, life as a founder would be much easier.

Ideas are journeys, not destinations. A startup idea isn't really something you *have*; it's something you create by working on it. If you wait until you have the perfect idea, you've misunderstood what it means to be a founder. The specifics of your idea will change and evolve. All you need to know initially is the area in which you are best suited to build, where you have a right to win (which we will discuss in depth later on).

The ideation framework we'll teach you revolves around discovering how your Edge – the combined experiences, skills and strengths of the founding team – influences the ideas co-founders can work on together. Working from your Edge – your specific, personal, competitive advantage – flips the notion that ideation involves whiteboarding a long list of big markets or interesting problems to solve. The key is to formulate a shared sense of what ideas you might be uniquely well placed to work on and then connect with customers who will allow you to experiment with, iterate and improve that idea over time.

A startup idea is a set of beliefs about how the world could and should be better. It's the opposite of static. Indeed, if you succeed, it will evolve and change, sometimes dramatically. Now, Apple was once an idea about a better personal computer. Google was an idea about a better search algorithm. Canva was an idea about how to easily design yearbooks. You can still see the imprints of these ideas in what these companies are today, but there's no meaningful sense in which they *are* those ideas. The ideas tech giants are based on have been tried, tested, iterated, refined and built – over and over again – until they became some of the most valuable entities in the world. These ideas are still in flux, even after decades of success. So, finding the perfect startup idea is a terrible hurdle to set yourself because ideas and what it takes to bring them to life are so dynamic.

Why is this concept of 'the right idea' so prevalent? Because most of us misunderstand the process of how new startups begin. A startup idea isn't a single eureka moment of insight or inspiration. It's the confluence of the right team, the right hunch and the right behaviours. Instead of spinning wheels trying to come up with the perfect idea in isolation, we recommend that entrepreneurs think of finding the right co-founder and selecting the right idea as the same process. You need to know something about yourself and what sorts of ideas might be a good fit for you to choose the right co-founder – who will in turn help shape the idea. (We'll cover co-founder fit and collaborative ideation later in this book.) An early-stage startup is a team of people, usually a co-founding pair, working on a hunch they have about something that should exist in the world. They test that hunch with other people who they think will use and buy that product – their customers.

Instead of testing and iterating, many aspiring founders fixate on figuring out everything that could possibly go wrong before they get started. They get too analytical too quickly. They ask their smart friends – who are not their target customers – to critique the idea. This is not the right test. Every idea – even the very best ones – have huge and glaring problems at the beginning. Think how ridiculous Airbnb or Uber could have been made to sound on Day One. If you're going to be working on one problem for a long time, it's much better to select a customer group you love and commit to making their lives better than to subject an initial idea to rigorous due diligence up front.

Other founders have the opposite problem: they think they have to fall madly in love with an idea before they can take the plunge. This can be a big mistake. In the early days, you are working hard to validate or invalidate an idea – and if you're in love with the idea, you might not be prepared to genuinely test and iterate it. For the founders we've worked with, so much about their idea changed, but what remained constant was the customer they served. They iterated into a better problem-solution fit for that customer. This made them more resilient founders.

Chapter Summary

People with incredible founder potential hold themselves back when they buy into myths and outmoded concepts of who can be a founder.

- The world is missing out on some of its best potential founders, due to cultural norms and misconceptions about what you must have to become a founder.
- Most people will talk about becoming a founder, but will find multiple reasons as to why now isn't the right time. This is an easy trap to fall into.

- Advanced credentials and perfect ideas do not pave the path to guaranteed entrepreneurial success.
- Developing a network around your idea is more important than starting with a big network.
- Fitting the 'typical' founder profile and being based in Silicon Valley is less important than ever.

CHAPTER 3

What Causes Failure and How to Avoid It

Founders usually talk about startup failure as something that happens to companies. They're the victim of some external, destructive force. But, in our experience, failure is less likely to come from a powerful storm knocking out the power than it is from the founder pulling the plug.

It's worth understanding the most common causes of panic and what you can do to avoid them. We find these tend to be non-obvious for most first-time founders; in fact, they're often the opposite of many entrepreneurs' intuitions. Founders need to be able to recognize the difference between hitting an obstacle and an endpoint, but you shouldn't fixate on failure. You need to plan to succeed.

Before you embark on this journey, you might think that failure looks like losing a co-founder or a whole team, starting your product again from scratch, changing ideas, losing your first and/or biggest customer, being told your idea is terrible, not getting the opportunity to pitch, not getting interest from investors or running out of money. But you'd be wrong. These obstacles aren't failures if they don't stop you. The successful companies we've worked with have collectively experienced them all.

Despite encountering these difficult situations, they didn't give up. They adapted their ideas. They rebuilt their teams. They dedicated themselves to customer development. They didn't cease to be founders. For the most part, things that look like failure in the early stages are just learning opportunities. Most startups fail at this very early stage because the founders give up too quickly and stop trying to find alternatives. Anything short of that isn't actually failure.

So, why do founders quit? Nearly all instances of failure *look* like they come from a lack of three critical resources: money, time or willpower. Yet we've seen many founders run out of money or time and still find a way to keep going. *The truth is that almost all failure as a founder is rooted in a lack of willpower.* Lack of the other two resources is just a proximate cause that sometimes leads them to walk away.

Money

Running out of money is deeply unpleasant. Similarly, worrying about money not only feels awful, but it makes you less effective. It's hard to concentrate on anything else if you're thinking about how to pay the bills. We don't want to trivialize the importance of money.

That said, running out of funds isn't necessarily a death sentence for your founding ambitions. If you're absolutely determined to continue, there's almost always a way to do so. We've coached teams that have bootstrapped for eighteen months with no external investment. Some founders have chosen to move to other cities or sleep on couches for months to reduce rent. We're not suggesting that these extreme approaches are mandatory, but there are many ways to adjust your lifestyle to keep the company running. It's very rare for startups to become bankrupt at the beginning. Obviously, it's possible. But unless you enter contracts that require you to pay large sums each month, you should be able to flex most costs.

When a founder quits because they've run out of money, it's usually because they don't want to make those trade-offs anymore. And that's fine. No one wants to be the founder who clings on for decades, scraping by on ramen noodles and their friends' sofas, always believing that they are one more iteration from glory but never quite getting there. At some point, quitting is rational. The problem, though, is reaching this point before you truly even start. As we noted earlier, for a founder of an early-stage company, quitting is almost *always* rational in the purely economic sense of maximizing income, even after you've made good progress.

To reiterate: if you're founding a startup because you think it's a good way to make a lot of money, think again. If you believe that, you've either been unaware of the empirical evidence on this point, or you might believe that *your* chances of success are much better than the average founder. We often call this 'personal exceptionalism'. A third alternative is that you put a very high premium on the identity of being a founder, irrespective of the outcome. That is, you'd rather be a poor(ish) founder than a rich(ish) banker.

Applying this framework to the problem of running out of money yields some interesting results. If founders quit when they decide that the economic trade-offs aren't worth it anymore, we can again say that one of three things is true. Either they didn't know the odds to begin with, they no longer believe that they are exceptional enough to shift the odds in their favour or they no longer place such a premium on being a founder. The first case is foolishness, and the latter two cases feel much more like running out of willpower than running out of money.

Time

Sometimes running out of time is equivalent to running out of money. For example, if you have to get traction or secure funding by a certain date to pay your rent or satisfy your financial backers, that's just a special case of running out of money.

In certain cases, you might have to pass up an opportunity to pitch because you're not ready to raise external funding yet. It's especially relevant for founders in accelerators. At Entrepreneur First, we host a 'Demo Day' towards the end of our programme, which is an opportunity to pitch to a room – physical or virtual – full of investors.

For the companies that are ready, it's a great opportunity to jumpstart fundraising. In terms of your startup's existence, a pitch date is an entirely artificial deadline. If you're committed to success, quitting because you weren't ready to talk to a particular audience on a predetermined date is pretty silly. Many of our teams have raised significant rounds of funding having never pitched at Demo Day. They may have missed the opportunity to present to a captive audience of investors, but they persevered and set up their own meetings when the time was right for them. This is a clear case where quitting because you're out of time really just means you're out of willpower.

Some founders also feel that they have a narrow window of time before competition comes along. But if another company enters your market, it's not the time to pack up. At this stage, competition rarely kills startups – at least not directly. The fundamental question is always, 'Can you build something that someone wants enough that they will pay for it?' If another company is already adequately providing what you had planned to build, the answer is 'no' from the beginning. But if the answer starts as 'yes', competition is unlikely to change that in the short term. Competition can only kill you in the long run, and a startup is doing really well by the time it ever reaches 'the long run'.

A deadline or some other time-crunch can also serve to focus your team. Perhaps you don't have the funds to go full-time with your startup right away, so you give yourself a certain number of months of runway building during nights and weekends before you make the leap.

Willpower

Willpower is the only resource that you can't afford to run out of during the early stage. Failure is often a choice; it's what happens when you stop trying. The good news is that there are several ways you can extend your reserves of willpower, just as there are ways to extend your financial runway when needed.

The first and easiest way is simply to internalize the fact that willpower is indeed a resource. You're much less likely to run out of money if you check your bank balance regularly, and you're less likely to run out of willpower if you're monitoring it. Once you acknowledge that deciding to quit is your biggest risk, you become much more wary of mindsets and behaviours that lead you in that direction. We'll talk more about this in the next chapter.

Practically, don't keep working on an idea or with people that don't give you energy. It's almost impossible to maintain willpower in those situations. We'll dive into some of these aspects in the next section of the book, but know that a founding team that can't generate an idea isn't working – you should break up as soon as possible. If you think your team is good, but it's not productive, again you're wrong. Break up now. Similarly, if the idea feels promising but the team isn't quite right, traction won't save you. You should break up now. It's sad, but it's common that when you fear the team isn't working, you're almost always right. Don't delay; you'll just use up willpower fruitlessly.

A related but distinct approach is to train yourself to competitively exercise willpower. Most of the entrepreneurs we work with are used to competing on dimensions of skill and talent. You measure yourself against peers and are irked when you find someone smarter, more skilled or more imaginative than you. Start noticing who might display more stamina and the traits and tricks they have for maintaining it. Marathon runners often look to align with a pacer who carries a sign with their target finish time on it. Staying in close proximity will keep a runner on track and steady, so they don't go out too fast and burn out quickly. Fellow entrepreneurs carry no such signs, but aligning yourself with a peer group, be it a cohort or online forum, can help you navigate the road ahead.

A third tactic to extend your willpower is to find a customer as early as possible. We'll elaborate on this at length later in the book. Finding someone who wants what you're selling isn't a one-off boost.

A customer who genuinely loves your product is someone you can go back to again and again – a living, breathing embodiment of why you're building the business. In our experience, very few startups that rapidly found a paying customer subsequently quit. Interestingly, the number of customers isn't important; even having a single person who will pay seems to be enough to keep a team's morale high. This means that you should almost always prioritize establishing your customer to the exclusion of all else.

Lastly, willpower wanes when you feel you don't know how to fill your time and you aren't generating the productive energy that helps propel you forward. We know a team is failing when the founders begin packing up at 6 p.m. every evening or spend long periods browsing Hacker News. They're not getting enough done, and, even worse, it suggests they're not motivated by what they're doing. The antidote is to set concrete, ambitious goals with very tight deadlines and strict check-ins. It's much harder to run out of willpower if you're driving hard toward a pre-agreed goal.

We structure our cohorts with built-in milestones, but if you're founding on your own, it's important to recognize that very early stages can be unpredictable, unplanned, unstructured (and even tedious). Assuming a lethargic pace right out the gate won't get you across the finish line. If you instead accept these realities and deliberately go at it with excitement, then you have better chances of building up enough knowledge, expertise and network in an area to generate real energy.

Founding a startup is a marathon up a mountain with very few encouraging spectators along the path. There are points when the clichéd cheer, 'Don't give up!' could even seem cruel. It's a platitude that makes people blame themselves for failure in an environment over which they have little control. However, as advice for founders, 'Don't give up!' is different. It's a reminder that whatever obstacle you've reached likely isn't the end of the road. You can choose to take yourself out of the race, but remember that it is a choice.

"There are going to be plenty of moments where most rational human beings will probably give up,' said EF investor Taavet Hinrikus. As the first employee at Skype, Hinrikus was part of the team from napkin sketch to reaching more than 100 million customers. He went on to co-found TransferWise (now Wise), a publicly traded, multi-billion dollar fintech company. He said that transitioning from employee to founder is like captaining a sailboat of which you were once a crew member. When a storm comes, you're the one responsible.

'My experiences from Skype showed me it's not easy, and there are many ways that startups can die,' Hinrikus said. 'When I left Skype, we were signing up 200,000 new users a day. When we launched TransferWise, we got seventy new users in a month. But when you're doing it yourself, it's your baby. You need to try ten times harder than as an employee; you need to put in ten times more tries to see if it works.'

Hinrikus feels tenacity and intensity are two characteristics that keep the best founders moving forward. Seeing what was possible during his time at Skype gave him a hunger to compete and inspired a framework for building a successful product.

'You can't have a ten per cent better service and win market share,' Hinrikus says. 'You need a ten times better service to actually get people to switch over because the switching cost is so big. Just being ten per cent better doesn't justify it.'

Enthusiastic early customer feedback and continuous growth kept him from quitting. Understanding what it would take to outpace the competition helped Wise win.

Failure is an unpleasant idea and a distressing experience. Realizing that it's something over which you have a degree of control may not make it any more palatable. Of course, there are points when it makes sense to walk away or pull the plug. We'll address the difference between drive and delusion later. But there are many situations when what might feel like a dead end simply requires a pivot. Steeling yourself against giving up is the most useful thing you can do as you found a company. As we've seen many times now, if you can put off The End just a few weeks longer, you often find that failure is no longer looming quite so large on the horizon.

Chapter Summary

Understanding the true cause of failure will help you see the difference between a setback and a dead end.

- Running out of resources can prompt a problem-solving pivot.
- Monitoring your internal willpower is as critical as knowing the amount in your bank account.
- You may encounter multiple failures and rebound, but quitting is a choice, not a result.

CHAPTER 4

Cultivating the Mindset of a Founder

Before we dive into some of the frameworks and methods we recommend for selecting an idea or choosing a co-founder, we need to talk about getting psychologically prepared to start a company. We have seen the impact that certain mindsets have on a founder's success and started working with a psychologist who specializes in the founder mindset. Gena Gorlin, PhD, is a professor and licensed psychologist who specializes in 'self-creators' – ambitious, independent-minded innovators pushing to make the most of their lives. She's worked with countless entrepreneurs – and is married to one.

In her practice and research, Gorlin has uncovered patterns in the attitudes self-creators need to have when addressing challenges. She advises founders to pay attention to the messages they're telling themselves. Certain mindsets can fuel behaviours that lead to success, and others can derail you. We've merged some of our own observations with Gena's advice on helpful vs hurtful founder mindsets. Go to howtobeafounder.com to see more of Gorlin's insights and advice.

Founders must have a rock-solid relationship with reality, and this includes practising radical self-honesty

The biggest bet you make as a founder is on the soundness of your independent judgement. You need to be able to identify when to follow your own opinion versus listening to the judgement and opinions of others. If you are creating something that hasn't existed before, it's likely you will have significant pushback from others. Some of this will be valid and useful, others you need to disregard.

Developing sound judgement is really hard work – especially given how easily we can deceive ourselves into feeling as if we've done that work. As psychology research has demonstrated, we are adept at seeing things as we wish they were, not as they truly are. For instance, we might tell ourselves we have done enough customer calls to validate our hunch when we know, on some level, that we have selectively chosen the easy targets and avoided the tougher ones. Or we might talk ourselves into believing that our really ambiguous idea will never work when, in fact, we are just afraid of all the uncertainty and rejection we might have to face if we take it on.

As Gorlin said, 'Another common category of lies we tell ourselves involves sunk cost. Once you've already poured time and energy into an idea, once you've become excited about it, once you've told all your friends and family about it, it becomes really painful to give it up – and increasingly so the farther you get.'

Sunk cost causes you to settle on the wrong idea or co-founder. If you're overly invested in a particular outcome, you become blind to the indicators that you're going in the wrong direction. We practice self-deception to protect ourselves from feeling the pain of failure. But by refusing to listen to the signals, we set ourselves up to fail. Gorlin said, 'It should hurt when you fail, but it shouldn't discourage or demoralize you. Failure is inherent in this process, and the higher you set your sights, the more times you're going to fall.'

If you know that certain contexts make it harder for you to be honest about your judgement of an idea or to let go of an idea, Gorlin recommends you try to minimize those triggers. You shouldn't tell too many friends about your idea if that's going to make it harder for you to later admit to a false start.

Rather than broadcasting your big goal to 'become a founder' broadly, research shows ambitious people should make 'implementation intentions' that focus on smaller, specific step-by-step planning goals. (Such as: This weekend, I will reach out to three people in my LinkedIn network who might be potential co-founders.) This keeps your brain's goal mindset active and helps you avoid the premature dopamine hit you'd get from all your contacts congratulating you on going after your dream. Implementation intentions create accountability to the behaviour needed to achieve your major ambition.

Another common trigger for self-deception is when we feel we need to downplay the potential holes and uncertainties in our vision in order to convince investors or other stakeholders to come on board. When you're bringing a new vision into reality, you're constantly selling. Partly so that you have fellow co-founders and team members to work with but also often your family and friends so that they buy into and legitimize your chosen career path. To do this right, we need to sensitize ourselves to the difference between 1) trying to 'sell people' on a B.S. version of reality – which will only set us up for a loss of credibility over time – versus 2) doing the work to help people see what we see (including our vision of what can be built and how it can change the world for the better). To sustain this latter kind of conviction, and convince other people to join you in it, you need to really see it – meaning it needs to be grounded in evidence, earned expertise and sound, careful reasoning, and to credibly capture the uncertainties and error margins involved. Inspiring conviction is forged through radical self-honesty, not through self-deception.

Instead of seeking validation from others, entrepreneurs need to build this mental muscle of radical self-honesty, the kind of self-awareness that allows you to examine and reflect on your own flaws, failings and strengths and take accurate stock of what you do and do not know. You no longer have a boss or performance review process that is going to give you an outside perspective. One way to do this is to make sure you carve out a place for introspection that stands apart from the pressure to pitch or sell to an audience. This might be with a friend, a family member, a coach or even just a personal journal. Create space where you can – without judgement – acknowledge your fears, work out worst-case scenarios and articulate upsides.

Being a founder is an opportunity to push yourself and others to greatness. It can be the most fulfilling and challenging path you take for both your career and your life. It's important to remember that 'It never ceases to be a choice', as Gorlin says. Part of radical self-honesty is reminding yourself that you have chosen to take this path. You can choose to continue, and you can choose to stop. As we talked about in the previous chapter, willpower is your most important resource and this reminder can create great resilience. A startup isn't something that is being done to you; it's something you choose to do because you believe this is the best way for you to have the kind of impact you want to have on the world.

Founders make the leap to execute their vision

When you found a tech company, you can be overwhelmed by the gap between what you need to bring into reality and what exists today. One of the solutions is to imagine the answer, create a prototype and sell that first (you'll find more on this in the Customer Development chapter later).

The problem arises when founders lose touch with which elements of the prototype are a reality and which elements are still a vision. Founders can get carried away by the vision. Their prototype then disappoints because they can't deliver what they've promised to customers, investors and employees. This can lead to unethical behaviour with disastrous consequences (such as the Theranos founder Elizabeth Holmes, who fraudulently claimed to have developed revolutionary blood-testing technology).

In the early stage of being a founder, you must toggle between articulating your inspiring vision and communicating the gritty reality of where you are and what it's going to take to enact your vision. This is an important skill to develop. If you don't distinguish between which mode you're in, you risk not only over-promising and under-delivering, but also failing to plan how you will bridge the gap. Learning to bridge vision and reality will help get your team through the low moments and instil confidence in investors so you can get the resources you need to continue.

Founders work to attune themselves to their authentic judgement

Demonstrating authenticity isn't about wearing your heart on your sleeve and saying the first thing that comes to mind. 'It's about matching up our behaviour and our communication with our own best-considered judgement of who we want to be and what we care about,' Gorlin said.

Developing authenticity early on is essential. Once founders step outside their belief bubble and begin to share their vision with others, it gets pretty noisy. If you can't access your own independent and authentic judgement, you can get defensive or shut down when your ideas are challenged.

'It's really hard to be authentic given that we often lose sight of our own considered judgement,' Gorlin said. 'It takes a lot of work to reactivate parts of our perspective and knowledge that we get blinded to in the heat of emotion. Sometimes what that means is we yell and scream, and sometimes what it means is we withdraw and defer, and that's not really what our authentic judgement would dictate.'

Demonstrating authenticity might require pausing to remind yourself of the bigger picture and the longer timeframe. You've spoken to this person for a reason and trust their judgement; they might be teaching you something, and you don't know it yet. When you voice your frustration, do so in a way that conveys your respect for the person you're disagreeing with, but don't lose sight of your values, knowledge and judgement.

Founders can't plan to fail

In the normal course of life, most of us like to think through Plan A, Plan B, Plan Z – we prefer to have multiple ways to deal with adversity. But making 'backup plans' for the potential failure of your company is a mistake. If you start to focus on what will happen if it doesn't work, you will never succeed.

One of the key ingredients of success is your ability to attract resources to your company before you have a lot of proof points. You need to inspire investors so you can get the funds to hire a team. You'll need to convince great people to forgo other opportunities and come work with you. And you'll need to convince your customers that you can deliver something you've not yet built. If you don't see how it could come to fruition and believe that it will happen, why should they?

If you can't visualize what success looks like, it's not going to materialize on its own. You have to start with the end in mind. You must hold a strong vision of where you're going so you can leap over the massive credibility gap that exists early on. If you start by imagining what can go wrong, it becomes a self-fulfilling prophecy.

Founders who succeed are constantly planning for what the world will look like when they succeed: who they will hire, what deals they will close, what the product will look like, what the company will look like in ten years' time.

Broadly, what we find is that the founders who are most paranoid about failing are often most likely to fail. This is partly because they're manifesting it through their actions and decisions without even realizing it. It's a little like riding a bike and looking over your left shoulder instead of directly ahead. Without knowing it, you will inevitably start to veer off course. This sounds counterintuitive, but founders who fail are often the ones allocating a significant part of their problem-solving capacity to strategically avoiding failure. They take the safer option to minimize the downside of whatever decision they're making. They're hedging to fail rather than planning to succeed.

Great founders often take a 'burn your boats' approach. The phrase was popularized by the story of Hernán Cortés, who in 1519 landed on the shores of what is now Mexico. Today, historians agree that Cortés didn't burn the boats, but he did scuttle them – deliberately sinking his ships so his men could not turn back.[8]

Successful founders don't make plans for failing. They behave like someone setting out for new and difficult terrain. They don't give themselves options to back out. If you haven't burned your boats, you'll be tempted to turn back at the first roadblock. If you've burned the boats, you must find a way through the jungle. There are so many ways to fail, so if you don't assume that there is a way through, you will take everything that happens along the way as a reason to turn back.

Great founders orient themselves to grow

People with a 'fixed mindset' believe their basic qualities – such as intelligence or talent – are rigid traits that predict success or failure.[9] Instead of putting effort into developing these qualities, they spend their time demonstrating and documenting success and failure. They find it hard to approach the iterative process of refining an idea because it requires them to be vulnerable in front of customers as they test and learn. It can be helpful to think of each version of your product as a draft, instead of a bound book you pull from the shelf.

---

[8] Reynolds, Winston A. 'The Burning Ships of Hernán Cortés'. *Hispania* 42, no. 3 (1959): 317–24. https://doi.org/10.2307/335707
     Gasca, Peter. 'For Entrepreneurial Success, Burn Your Boats'. Inc.com, April 30, 2018. https://www.inc.com/peter-gasca/for-entrepreneurial-success-burn-your-boats.html
[9] Dweck, C. (2017). *Mindset*. London: Robinson.

Just as a writer who wants to be published must revise and redraft a manuscript with the help of an editor, entrepreneurs should be listening to and integrating feedback from their customers as a key part of their process. If you wait until it's 'ready', you're unlikely to ever release a product.

On the other hand, founders who adopt a 'growth mindset' approach uncertain areas with curiosity. They believe they can cultivate skills, behaviours and attitudes. They are consummate learners.[10] They're able to process setbacks as learning opportunities rather than evidence that they don't have what it takes.

Suppose you think that you're not comfortable enough with rejection to be good at sales. A fixed mindset stops you right there. Maybe you try and fail. You process failure as being about *you* rather than being about learning. With a fixed mindset, you tell yourself that sales just isn't your thing. Someone with a growth mindset wonders, 'How am I going to learn?' You're going to read all the books on the subject. You're going to speak to people who know how to do it. You're going to practise on lower-value customers and work your way up as you hone your skills.

Think about being a founder as a career dedicated to learning. Reid Hoffman, founder of LinkedIn and investor at Greylock, says the best founders are 'infinite learners'. Whenever you think you know how to do something because you're on a high-growth path, you'll immediately become a newbie again. You're growing your team to thirty people and learning how to approach human resources. Then you're scaling your team to sixty people, which has its own set of challenges and considerations. It feels as though no sooner have you closed your first $10,000 customer, you're closing your first $100,000 customer – it's a completely different ballgame.

The best founders find satisfaction in learning. They constantly scale themselves with their companies. They see their role as making sure

10   Ibid.

that they can keep up – from a skills and ability perspective – with each growth phase of the company.

It's not unusual to suffer from imposter syndrome as a founder. Imposter syndrome can either hold you back or fuel your drive. Everyone has periods of doubting their abilities or feeling like a fraud. As a founder, you experience it so frequently because you're creating something new. It's not just that *you're* not the expert – in uncharted territory, no one is. If you're challenging the status quo in an industry, you're even more likely to feel self-doubt because you're thinking differently from everyone else around you.

If you have a fixed mindset, imposter syndrome is crippling. You feel you're not good enough, so you put up a facade of expertise instead of exposing yourself to the experiences that will allow you to develop. On the other hand, imposter syndrome in someone with a growth mindset can be an advantage. Your discomfort in a situation flags a lack of expertise and prompts you to figure out *how* you're going to learn.

As one of the founders we have worked with said, 'I noticed a huge shift in my performance when I started to understand that my imposter syndrome was signalling two real positives. First, I've pushed myself into uncomfortable or exceptional opportunities. Second, I have enough awareness to identify situations where I'm out of my depth and need to go and spend some time learning. Once I'd made this switch, I became much more comfortable with uncertainty and willing to push on into more challenging contexts.'

As we said earlier, you can't reduce the risks of starting a company to zero, but cultivating the right mindsets not only makes you more likely to succeed but should also make the journey less stressful and more satisfying.

Chapter Summary

Founders are 'self-creators' who must develop keen self-awareness to effectively drive towards a vision.

- Founders need to practise radical self-honesty. This requires space for reflection.
- Plan for success. Don't plan to avoid failure. Fallback plans can sabotage founders.
- Espousing a growth mindset turns moments of failure into learning opportunities.

PART 2

The Founding Process

There is no fail-proof formula for building a startup. But the tested frameworks and helpful heuristics in these next chapters will keep you from fumbling around in the dark during the earliest stages. We walk through the same concepts we introduce to members in our selective cohorts, from defining your Edge to linear ideation.

Although our timelines are geared towards teams who are fully focused on founding, don't be discouraged if you can't afford to quit your job or are navigating the early stages while also caring for your family. In the ten years between founding Entrepreneur First and writing this book, our lives have drastically changed. The constant has been a commitment to our belief that the world is missing out on its best founders and our role in demystifying startup inception.

Our approach to founding may be different from anything you've read or heard before. We put a great deal of emphasis on what makes (and breaks!) a strong founding team. In our experience, the mix of strong interpersonal dynamics coupled with innovation creates a powerful force for propelling globally important companies. And the fuel that keeps great companies competitive is a genuine love for the customer. This section covers how to identify those 'hair-on-fire' early adopters, learn from them and build the best product possible.

CHAPTER 5

Three and a Half Rules for Ambitious Founders

There is no single formula for startup success. It's not paint-by-numbers. Industry nuances and unique co-founder experiences mean the path can look quite different from one team to the next. There are, however, a few rules we recommend all founders embrace. We encourage founders to think in terms of three principles that will nudge you towards building a company that fulfils your potential and ambition. There are in fact three and a half rules – the 'half rule', as you'll see, is one that we believe strongly, but that we know isn't for everyone.

Rule 1: Scale Matters

As an ambitious person, there are many ways you might choose to realize your aspirations. Starting a company is one of the best ways to accomplish your goals. But because of the extraordinary amount of effort it takes to found and grow a startup, it doesn't make sense to choose this path unless you truly desire to be a founder. And it is our belief that if you want to be a founder, you should set out to achieve a really big outcome.

The difficulty is that, unlike architects, there is no one-size-fits-all blueprint for founders to follow. Every business is different and will have a different outcome. Most of the time when entrepreneurs frame a 'big outcome', they're talking about money. Creating value for yourself is a good thing, but what about your customers, employees and investors? Others might define 'big outcome' as impact, through lives touched or severity of the problem solved. Whatever your motivation, the ability to scale is the foundation that will determine whether your company fulfils your ambition or merely scratches an itch. 'We have a lot of startups that aim to solve the founder's own personal problems, which sometimes could be consumer-related problems such as valet parking or grocery delivery. But there are many problems out there that, while not specifically one person's personal problem, are issues at national or global scale – things like food, water, agriculture and climate. And we don't have enough people solving those. If you go after those, you can start a very large, impactful, and successful company,' said Ali Tamaseb, venture capitalist and author of *Super Founders*.

With startups, effort isn't strongly correlated with outcome. In terms of stress and hours worked, it can be just as hard to build a small business as a big one. Go ask someone who's opened a bar or a café. Many of the challenges that plague entrepreneurs – worrying about cash flow, hiring and firing people, attracting and retaining customers – are going to be the same whether you're building a brick-and-mortar store or a software company. *The difference is that the payoff for all that stress is much bigger if you can find an idea that scales.* Scalability is the key to the unlimited upside that sets a founder apart from your shop owner or friend who owns a recruitment consultancy.

One note of caution about scale: it's critical that you choose the right metric to scale. It's easy to get seduced by what are often called 'vanity metrics'. These numbers might make you feel good about what you're doing, but they don't get to the core of what your company is about. For example, the number of employees might be a vanity metric. You can get a big ego boost by saying, 'I employ 200 people.' That might be great, but it says nothing about what they're doing or how much output they generate. Think of WhatsApp, which was acquired for $19bn while only having fifty-five employees. Vanity metrics can apply to capital, too. If you read the tech press, you'll see startups shouting from the rooftops about how much capital they've raised. Money can be really useful – that's true. But the flip side is that those founders just sold more of their company to investors, diluting their own equity.

It's great to have people if your employees are doing something very valuable. But ultimately, people are expensive. In the same way, it's great to have capital if you need a lot of money to scale, but capital is also expensive in terms of equity. This is why it's so important to avoid getting distracted by vanity metrics as you scale. The more useful way to measure your progress is to think about the unit of impact you're trying to achieve – for example, hours spent on the product – and scaling that as much as possible.

There are many ways to think about what scale means, but the single most important question to ask is this: How do you get out of the business of selling your time? Because if you are selling your time, you are always going to be the bottleneck. It's cliché because it's true – there are only a certain number of hours in a week. While it's possible to increase the value of your time and make incrementally more money, you eventually hit your limit. Scaling your product takes your time out of the equation. You can sell exponentially more units – and you are not the bottleneck.

The classic unscalable business is similar to a hairdresser. Now, there are some very expensive hairdressers out there. But ultimately, they are still selling their time. Even at their most ambitious, they have only seventy hours a week available. The only way to scale is to open a full salon, which remains limited by the team's bookable hours. If you execute well, you can make a decent profit as a salon owner. But your impact is limited to the people who sit in your chairs. Scale matters.

Rule 2: Be Ambitious From the Beginning

If you want to build a globally important company, you have to think big from the beginning. Often founders believe that if they lower their ambitions, they increase their odds of success. We believe the opposite. As we mentioned earlier, there's nothing easy about running a small business. But it's more than that – if you start with too small a vision, you're actually *more* likely to fail.

Perhaps that seems counterintuitive, but it's the consequence of a simple point about resources. There are two scarce resources that any startup needs to thrive: talent and capital. At least to begin with, a startup is the sum of the people in your team. To build an exceptional business, you need to hire exceptional people. And for that reason, if you want to grow fast, you'll likely need to raise capital. You need money to hire great people, pay the rent and buy the various products and services your business will require.

The important point is that both those resources – talent and capital – are attracted to ambition. Both talent and capital have a high opportunity cost. The sort of people you want to hire to make your company a success have lots of options – including starting their own company. How do you convince such people to work for you or invest in you – particularly at the beginning when you have little money and few tangible assets – when they could make a higher salary elsewhere or become a founder themselves? Pretty much all you have is your vision – the possibility that you're offering them a seat on a rocket ship. Faced with a set of job offers, brilliant people often choose the most ambitious one, even if it's not the best paid.

Similarly, venture capitalists have hundreds, sometimes thousands, of startups to pick from when deciding where to invest. As we'll discuss in more detail later, the VC business model only works if the fund can back companies that get *really* big – ideally, that become worth billions of dollars. And, of course, it's very unlikely that an unambitious idea will ever reach that level.

A lot of us have the intuition that a smaller, less ambitious idea is easier to execute, but this is because we forget that ease of execution is a function of the talent and capital we have at our disposal. It's *much* easier to succeed when both are readily available. But they're only available, generally, to ambitious founders and companies, so it's better to bake in ambition from the start.

Rule 3: Be a Missionary *and* a Mercenary

It's quite popular in VC circles to divide founders into two groups – missionaries versus mercenaries. The basic idea is that mercenaries are out to make a lot of money – they spot an opportunity or a 'gap in the market' and go after it – while missionaries are zealously motivated to solve a particular problem. Conventional wisdom is that missionaries create more valuable companies because they're more resilient and determined, focus on the long term and can better attract talent.

In our experience, it's a false dichotomy – you need to have characteristics of both to be a successful founder.

The best founders are missionaries in that they can build a belief and vision around the problem they're trying to solve. They're motivated and enthusiastic enough about the idea to convince other people to go along with them. But they're also mercenary enough to be willing to adapt the idea and change tack when the customer tells them they're heading in the wrong direction. The risk for founders who are *too* missionary is that they keep going in the wrong direction despite that feedback because they aren't willing to let go of their vision. You need to be missionary enough to care but mercenary enough to respond to signals from the market.

In the book *Super Founders*, Ali Tamaseb looks at all of the billion-dollar companies founded over the last twenty years and finds that there were no significant differences in outcome between so-called missionaries and mercenaries. He notes founders often feel pressure to fake missionary zeal, even if they've just stumbled into something that looks like it might be lucrative.

This itself is a risk. It's hard to run a company for any length of time if you can't be your authentic self while doing so. We recommend that you're ruthlessly honest about your motivations. *What am I willing to invest my life in? What will excite me? What will make me come alive?* Are you attracted to starting a company for its own sake or to solve a specific problem?

We strongly recommend that you only start a company where you care deeply about the customer. Founders working in markets and with customers in whom they don't have a particular interest often struggle. Even if they gain some initial traction, it's easy to burn out and give up when the going gets tough.

One of our favourite examples of a mission-driven company is AccuRx, now one of the UK's biggest healthtech companies. They provide mission-critical patient–doctor communication services to over 98 per cent of the UK's primary care doctors. Their dedication to their mission has been a key ingredient in their success. But what they have today isn't the first version of the idea they worked on. They originally set out to build software to help doctors prescribe drugs more effectively. They struggled to get traction for the first product they built, so they started working on a different problem for the same customer. They were missionary about the customer, not about the specific idea. It was because they believed deeply that there was a big role for technology to play in improving the lives of patients and doctors that they iterated through until they found something that worked – and once they did, it worked spectacularly.

One final note of caution: as we've said, one danger for early-stage founders is feeling a deep sense of mission towards an *idea* for which there's no demand. The key, instead, is to be missionary about your *customer*, as we'll discuss in more detail later. You need to keep the mercenary side of your brain switched on to be constantly alert to signals about what your customers want and will ultimately pay for. But if you don't also leave space for your missionary side, you'll likely find yourself exhausted and lacking direction. The best founders combine the zeal of a missionary and the agility of a mercenary.

Rule 3.5: All Other Things Equal, Start a Software Company

As we'll discuss in the chapters to come, there's no such thing as a universal 'good idea'. You have to find the idea that's the best fit for you. This might lead you to all sorts of places. At Entrepreneur First, we've funded everything from rocket engines to lab-grown shrimp. That's why this is only half a rule. It doesn't apply to everyone. That said, we do have a strong view that, all other things equal, you should start a software company.[11] Software is the pinnacle of scalability. You are not selling your time; you're selling a copy of a program. Whether you sell one copy or a billion copies, most of the work is done in the initial build.

Entrepreneurship built on digital technologies – software, the internet, mobile phones, artificial intelligence and the like – represents the most powerful 'technology of ambition' yet. There are four big reasons why internet-enabled software businesses are the closest thing the world has seen to the perfect business model.

First, **reach**. If you can deliver your product over an internet connection, you have the potential to reach and impact more people than has ever been possible before. This should feel irresistible whether you're an altruist or a megalomaniac. Napoleon would be green with envy at the scale of influence Mark Zuckerberg commands today. For the first time in history, you can build a product from your bedroom that touches the lives of billions of people each day.

Second, **scope**. There's almost no area of human life where software doesn't have a role to play. As Marc Andreessen – co-founder of VC firm Andreessen Horowitz – says, software is eating the world. For example, traditional taxis and hotels are hardly considered high-tech. But today, the most important companies in both sectors are

---

[11] We know we didn't follow our own advice here – and we often wish we had, particularly as we scaled Entrepreneur First.

technology companies: Uber and Airbnb. This means that even people with no intrinsic interest in technology itself can and will turn to digital technologies to realize their goals.

Third, **cost**. The cost of starting (if not scaling) a technology company has collapsed over the past decade. The ability to reuse open-source code and rent computational power in the cloud has been a game-changer for the accessibility of entrepreneurship. Founders who started internet companies in the 1990s had to raise over a million dollars *before* Day One to be able to buy the physical servers on which their products would run. Today, Amazon and Microsoft will compete to give you free cloud computing credits (at least to begin with...). It's not much of an exaggeration to say that if you can afford a laptop, you can afford to start a software company.

Finally, **economics**. Software businesses have a truly beautiful property: zero marginal cost. That means – while it might cost a lot of money to design and build the product – once you've done it, each additional unit you sell costs you (almost) nothing – so your average cost per unit *falls* as you scale. Most businesses are not like this: the millionth serving of a restaurant meal or item of clothing costs you more or less the same to make as the first. It's this characteristic that makes software so scalable – and is one reason that so many of the world's most valuable companies are, at heart, software businesses.

So, if you consider the spectrum – on one end, a hairdresser, on the other end, a software company – you want to push as far towards the scalable side of that spectrum as possible. This means you need to be willing to make a big up-front time investment to make a product that you can sell many times over at relatively low marginal effort for the individual sale. Venture capital is designed to support this kind of business by providing the capital for this initial design and build period before the company can generate revenue.

So far, we've given general advice for founders – designed to help you figure out if it's the right path for you and give you the foundations for success – but now we're ready to get specific. How can you actually get started?

Chapter Summary

Embracing these principles isn't a formula for success, but it is fundamental for ambitious founders:

- Creating a startup is hard, regardless of its size. Scalability (especially through software) is the key to realizing unlimited upside on your business inputs.
- Don't temper your ambition. Plotting an ambitious trajectory from the outset will help you attract capital and talent.
- Combine missionary and mercenary mindsets and put the customer at the centre.

CHAPTER 6

Understand Your Edge

In 2013, we made a decision that might have been the most expensive mistake of our lives. We were interviewing a prospective founder for admission to Entrepreneur First. He was smart, driven, unconventional – all the things that we look for in founders, as we discussed earlier. We turned him down. That person, Alex Dalyac, went on to start a groundbreaking company called Tractable that at the time of writing is worth over a billion dollars.

Fortunately for us, Alex *did* start his company at Entrepreneur First – but a year later, having gone away and re-applied. He tells us now that our rejection the first time around was one of the most valuable things that ever happened to him, without which Tractable wouldn't exist.

So why did we turn him down, and why did he come back? Alex had all the *general* characteristics we think make for a great entrepreneur. Indeed, they're part of what has made him and Tractable so successful today. But in 2013, he lacked something that we consider essential – something we call 'Edge'.

Your Edge is a specific, personal, competitive advantage – the thing you bring to the table that is the foundation of a great idea and co-founding team. After we said no, Alex went away and completed a one-year degree in artificial intelligence, with a focus on what was a cutting-edge branch of the discipline called 'deep learning'. This became his Edge. He wasn't a world expert by the end of that year, of course, but he did know enough to have a clear sense of how deep learning could be the basis of a disruptive technology company –

and enough to attract a co-founder with a world-class research background in the space. Today, Tractable is one of the world's most valuable AI startups. Deep learning is still the basis of the technology that allows them to serve millions of insurance customers around the world each year.

If you enter the world of startups and investing, you'll hear the same phrase time and time again: 'Building a company is one of the hardest things you'll ever do.' We'd take this one step further – in many ways, building a company is a totally irrational thing to do. When it comes to creating a globally important, profitable startup, the statistical likelihood of success is incredibly small. As a startup founder, the odds are stacked against you from Day One. For all the Airbnbs, Snapchats and Tractables, there are thousands of startups that never make it. Many of these are good ideas built by smart people. But the uncomfortable reality is that entrepreneurship is a high-risk, high-reward career path – most people who try will fail. In the startup ecosystem, the winners are always the edge cases.

After helping hundreds of individuals attempt to start a company, we started spotting patterns, tracking data and asking questions. Why was it that even the smartest people were failing? How could ideas that made so much sense lose momentum so soon? Over time, we realized that the power wasn't in shaping the outputs or making the ideas 'better'. It was in changing the **inputs**. This meant focusing on the foundation from which ideas came.

We have seen that startups with the strongest founder-idea fit are most likely to succeed. Success comes as a result of two founders, their fit with each other, and their fit with the idea they pursue. You cannot separate these. Ideation and team-building need to happen simultaneously. The best founders realize that finding a co-founder and an idea is a symbiotic process.

It was clear that we needed to come up with a different way to help founders create globally impactful companies. We needed a framework that could underpin the two foundational pillars of building a startup

– the co-founding team and the idea – and that acknowledged the power of developing them in parallel. After helping thousands of individuals around the world start a company, we developed the concept of Edge.

Understanding Your Edge

Your Edge is your deepest knowledge, behaviours or skills. Using your Edge means leveraging these assets that you *already* have to fast-track the founding process. Edge is about understanding yourself and practising self-honesty about your strengths. By understanding yourself and what you can bring to an idea and a team, you can better seek out and communicate what you're looking for in a co-founder.

You probably have multiple Edges, so it can be helpful to think of your Edge as a hand of playing cards. Your cards are made up of the skills, expertise, experience and networks you already have. Each will have a different value. You need to know the cards in your hand and the strength of those cards in relation to each other and other people.

We designed Edge for individuals with relatively little experience to help them find a starting point. However, we have since found that our Edge framework helps potential founders regardless of the stage of their career.

How to find your Edges

Edge is not complex, but it can be counterintuitive. The process of finding your Edges requires you to define your most valuable skills, behaviours or areas of expertise. Our simple Edge framework will help you tease out areas where you might have spent time during work or academia. You then use your Edge as a starting point to find a problem that you're uniquely suited to solve and for finding a co-founder whose Edges intersect with yours. This is how you get to founder-idea fit.

Types of Edge

There are three kinds of Edge that cover your commercial experience (Market Edge), your skills (Tech Edge) and behaviours (Catalyst Edge). You will likely have some experience or skills across all three. As you go through the framework, you should think about which of these Edges might be strongest and how you would compare the strength of your different Edges.

Edge types

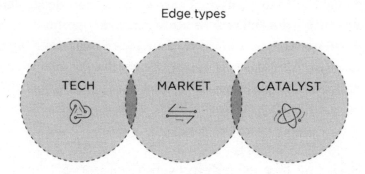

Generally, the successful founders we've worked with were particularly strong on one of these three types of Edge. Identifying your strongest Edge, or primary Edge, can help you kick off conversations with potential co-founders and assign roles at the outset of your partnership.

1. Market Edge

If you have experience working within a particular industry and have an insight into its big challenges and opportunities, you are likely to have a Market Edge. What you're looking for is *sufficient* experience in a particular market. You have seen the status quo and become incredulous enough to want to challenge it.

Whitney Wolfe Herd, founder of the dating app Bumble, started her multi-billion-dollar company at twenty-five using her Market Edge. Wolfe Herd was previously on the founding team of Tinder where she observed what didn't work well, both on the app and in her workplace. Her experiences contributed to forming her Edge: on Bumble, women talk first to set an equal tone from the start. Many individuals have experienced the ineffectiveness of dating apps, but Wolfe Herd had a strong Edge because she understood the market.

Key components of a Market Edge are:

- **Sufficient market knowledge**. Enough familiarity with how and why an industry works the way it does to understand how it might need to change. Extensive market knowledge, on the other hand, can dull your ability to perceive opportunities. After about six years in a given market, you're more likely to have accepted the status quo. Helen Murphy, co-founder of Opply in London, spent almost five years working at global FMCG company Procter & Gamble. There she had gained a knowledge of how supply chains work and she was able to use this as the foundation for Opply.

- **Insight on how the industry can be improved**. Your insight should be non-obvious. It should be surprising. Ask yourself: 'What did I find most ineffective or shocking when I first joined the industry?' *Would someone outside of the industry have intuited this?* If yes, you need to go back to the drawing board. For example, Pramod Ghadge, co-founder of Unbox Robotics in Bangalore, had been deploying robots in Flipkart warehouses and realized they were built for horizontal floor plans. This might work for wide greenfield warehouses for traditional supply chains, but in regions such as India with growing eCommerce demand, the package distribution and delivery necessitates using the least amount of real estate, ideally within the city limits. He could see there was a clear need for vertical package sorting systems, which would be a completely different value proposition.

In startups, we see something of a bell curve around experience and suitability to start a company. Just as it's unlikely (but not impossible) for someone with no market knowledge at all to have enough of an Edge to succeed, it is also pretty rare that the right person to disrupt an industry has had a successful thirty-year career in the space. There's a point at which that experience becomes a *disadvantage*. You know everything that can go wrong. You just can't imagine how anything could ever be any different. You've seen it all, and it's given you experience blindness.

When we first met our now-investor Reid Hoffman, he shared that the biggest investing mistake he'd made was passing on the early funding rounds of the payment company Stripe. Hoffman had been a founding board member of PayPal, and because of his deep experience with payments, he told us that he got hung up on all the ways the startup might fail. It turned out that he knew too much. In 2021, Stripe raised a $600 million round of funding at a valuation of $95 billion and became the most valuable privately held startup in the US.

One of the reasons why people underrate their readiness to start companies is they often think they need decades of experience. They feel they need expert knowledge of every element of the industry. The evidence suggests that's not necessary. **Industries get disrupted by people who know enough to be dangerous.** You need *sufficient* experience. Sufficient experience means that you have seen the status quo, but you haven't become so entrenched that you have become part of it. It's worth remembering that a little over 50 per cent of founding CEOs of billion-dollar companies had less than a year's worth of relevant work experience before starting their companies. It's striking how often successful founders say things like, 'If I'd known how hard it would be, maybe I wouldn't have started.' A degree of 'naive optimism' is sometimes what's needed to tackle big problems that your more knowledgeable counterparts might not even consider.

Take Aaron Levie. He used observations from his internship at Paramount Pictures and how his university handled file sharing as the initial idea for Box – which he founded straight out of university.

Barney Hussey-Yeo – who founded Cleo, a leading financial advice app for millennials and Gen Z – had eighteen months' work experience at London's biggest fintech startup before he became an entrepreneur. Was he a finance expert? No. But he'd had enough exposure helping people manage their money to understand the status quo and how it could change. The network he built also proved highly valuable – the founder of the company he worked for, Errol Damelin, went on to be one of his seed investors.

2. Technical Edge

At Entrepreneur First, we invest primarily in software startups, some of which have cutting-edge technology at their core. This means that most of the companies in our portfolio have someone with a Technical Edge on the co-founding team (although of varying strengths). Founders with a Technical Edge often, but not always, become the CTO.

Founders with Technical Edges have expertise with a specific technology. There are multiple ways to develop this. Some are formal, such as through academia or working as a developer in a big tech company. Others come from obsessional learning outside traditional structures – examples might include being deeply embedded in an online community dedicated to a particular technology or contributing to an open-source software project. Founders with a Technical Edge typically want to apply their skills to hard, real-world problems – even if they're not yet sure of the specific problem they want to solve. Sandy Lerner, the co-founder of Cisco Systems, is a great example of someone with a Tech Edge. She was able to use her master's degree in statistics and computer science from Stanford University to create the first router.

It's worth noting that having a Tech Edge doesn't mean that you have to be a CTO; there's no reason you couldn't take on the role of CEO in a co-founding team. CEO is a role, not a persona, and you can read more about the work of a CEO in Chapter Three. Founders who have a Tech Edge, such as the Collison brothers who founded Stripe (and invested in Entrepreneur First), have built some of the world's most valuable companies.

Key components of a Tech Edge are:

- **The compulsion to push boundaries and solve problems**. Individuals with Tech Edges are compulsive builders and creators. They want to build something that hasn't existed before and have many examples of trying to do this in the past, through side projects for example. They build with intent, often inspired by solving real problems. Take Harry Conor Lucas, co-founder of Phasio, who developed a SaaS product while still at university in Australia to help vineyards predict grape yield. What started as a side project turned into his first startup and raised $100,000.

And, either

- **Differentiated technical expertise that you want to apply to real-world problems**. You may feel as though you're surrounded by people who know more about this technology than you do, particularly if you have an academic background. Ask yourself: 'How many of these people are building startups?' You aren't comparing your technical ability to your lab or workmates; you're comparing it to the rest of the founder population. For example, Trisha Chatterjee, co-founder of immunitoAI in Singapore, developed her deep expertise in machine learning. She did this first through her master's degree in computer science and then through her career in the industry applying AI to real-world problems, such as in logistics and advertisement.

Or

- **Practical technical skills that allow you to build a product fast**. You have been building products and side projects since you were a kid. You have the skills to bring ideas to life in code and the desire to get them in front of customers. Such as Tomide Adesanmi, co-founder of Circuit Mind in London, who has always relentlessly created side projects – such as a mobile app for finding short videos that had thousands of users and a programmable 3D light cube that he used to teach kids to code at nationwide workshops.

As someone with a Tech Edge, you are obsessed with technologies and products. If you've gone down the academic track, you might love elements of your work but be frustrated by the barriers to real-world impact you face in your current environment. You want to apply your research findings, not wait for them to be published in a paper in hopes that someone else will act on them. If you're in industry, you might feel stymied by your company's priorities and see a much bigger opportunity. You want to explore your technology's full potential for impact in the world. You likely have a strong growth mindset where you're constantly striving to improve, like Shi Ling Tai, co-founder of Singapore-based UI-licious. She said, 'I was not born a genius programmer; I have worked really hard to get to where I am in the mastery of the craft. Calling it talent makes my efforts look cheap.'

3. Catalyst Edge

Most great startups have a founder with a Catalyst Edge. The Catalyst Edge is a set of behaviours that drive forward high-performance startups. If you have a Catalyst Edge, you will excel at recognizing and appreciating the Edge of your co-founder and seeing that it can be transformed into a fledgling company. Steve Jobs is perhaps the ultimate example: his partner Steve Wozniak had an extraordinary Tech Edge, but it required Jobs's energy and vision to create Apple.

Unlike the other two Edges, a Catalyst Edge tends to show up more in behaviour than experience or skills. Founders with a Catalyst Edge tend to have multiple examples of making things happen, of acts of extraordinary persuasion and building and motivating teams. Their role is not only to get things done but to amplify and commercialize the expertise of their teammates. One analogy we find useful to understand Catalysts is to think about the role of the screenwriter compared to the director. Phoebe Waller-Bridge can write compelling stories about being a woman in her twenties. Director Harry Bradbeer doesn't need to have had those experiences to bring them to life. His behaviours and skills allow him to catalyse the story into a five-time Emmy Award-winning TV show – *Fleabag*.

Key components of a Catalyst Edge are:

- **A track record of achievement and intense curiosity**. As a Catalyst, you're insanely productive. Have you already excelled in multiple different fields? Do you enjoy learning about new and challenging problems and thinking about how to solve them?
- **Strong commerciality.** The most successful individuals who have a Catalyst Edge are obsessed with creating value for their customers and then working out how their company can capture part of that value. They are obsessed with what customers want and fascinated by business models. This enables Catalyst Edges to interrogate and unlock the potential value of a new technology or market insight. (This doesn't mean that you need years of commercial experience; we've worked with many younger founders who just seem to have a 'knack' for this, usually borne out of relentless curiosity.)
- **Excellent communication and product mindset.** Relative to the experience of founders with a Market or Technical Edge, the interpersonal skills, strategic thinking and commercial acumen of the Catalyst Edge might seem 'soft' skills. But these competencies have helped propel some of the most highly valued companies in the world. Those with a Catalyst Edge are often the spokesperson for a company – they may need to serve as a translator between the deep specialization of a founder with a Technical Edge and

the outside world of investors and customers. Catalysts are often also product thinkers who consistently prioritize the needs of their customers or users. They anchor their team to solving their customer's problems.

- **Ability to 'adopt the spots' of their co-founder**. Do you find it easy to become an expert in new areas very quickly? Those with a Catalyst Edge are able to absorb knowledge around their co-founder's Edge. They rapidly assimilate the language and vocabulary of the field such that they often seem to have far more experience than they actually do. They are chameleons. They can present with confidence but demonstrate a lifelong learner's humility.

We observe that founders with a Catalyst Edge often display a certain restlessness before they start their companies. They're constantly seeking out new growth opportunities and the right opportunity to throw their relentless energy into.

Founders with a Catalyst Edge come from a wide range of backgrounds, but some common paths we see include being an early employee in a startup, working in high-ambition roles in financial or professional services or developing their own products in their spare time. They're competitive, hard-working, ambitious and never quite satisfied – they just need the right outlet for their potential. Catalysts possess a rare combination of characteristics and behaviours. **They move fast with purpose.**

To bring this to life, look at Jesse Shemen, co-founder of Papercup, who started his career at Deloitte as an analyst. He was soon agitating within the company and co-founded a new incubator and ventures arm inside it. Hélène Guillaume Pabis, founder of Wild.AI, had a successful career in finance as a Hedge Fund quant, played rugby semi-professionally, podiumed 100km ultra-marathons and is an ice-swimmer. Finally, Jacob Haddad, co-founder of AccuRx, aced his academic career, was student union president, set up a TEDx conference, was a first-aid responder at the London Olympics and was a finalist in a top TV cooking show.

Lara Hämmerle, co-founder of Hier Foods in Berlin, has a Catalyst Edge. She said:

> I just don't like losing, especially if I am responsible for it. This, paired with a tendency to rather pick the larger than the smaller battles, ends up being an ultimate intrinsic driver to me. I enjoy being at the forefront of change. I constantly look for room for improvement, analyse where and what to tweak and to ultimately reward myself by closely observing the impact. People give me energy. I want people around me; I want to develop them individually and build structures that help them act as a team to achieve whatever the goal is they set themselves. I just never stop getting joy from building things from the ground up.

Market and Tech Edges can give you an advantage in generating an idea while having a Catalyst Edge can give you an advantage in *executing* an idea. Many of the strongest CEOs we have worked with had a primary Catalyst Edge and used those behaviours to execute on their secondary Market or Tech Edges. If you take Jacob from the examples above, he had a secondary Market Edge having spent a year working in healthcare consulting. He was able to catalyse his light Market Edge to create the idea behind the company. AccuRx is now one of the fastest growing healthtech companies in the world.

Defining your Edge

Identifying your Edge is the crucial first step for a founder. Taking the time to understand how you can leverage your past experiences and behaviours can fast-track your founding process. To understand your

Edge, ask yourself a series of questions to help identify the experience, skills and behaviours *you already have*. Past behaviour is the best predictor of future behaviour. Look at how you've spent the majority of your productive hours. For most of us, that time is spent in our field of work or pursuing education. Your Edge is an area where you have developed insider experience, not a hobbyist's interest.

To understand what Edges you might have, and to what depth, answer the following questions:

Market Edge
- Where have you worked? What did you learn about that industry that would have surprised an outsider?
- When else have you had exposure to markets or industries that enabled you to learn about their idiosyncrasies and challenges?

Tech Edge
- What technologies do you have a particularly deep understanding of?
- Which technologies, that you have experience with, do you believe are under-commercialized?

Catalyst Edge
- When have you quickly assimilated into a new industry? When have you done this multiple times to a high level?
- When have you quickly built and commercialized prototype products?
- When was the last time you spotted an opportunity that wasn't obvious to others who had deeper knowledge of that industry?

You might find that you can only answer questions in one particular category. This means you have a very strong Primary Edge that will likely provide a focused starting place for building your startup. You might find that you have answers across all categories. That means there are many different areas you could potentially work on.

It can be useful to rank your Edges. This is a good mental model for understanding yourself and can be invaluable when you want to communicate your Edge to potential co-founders. For example, here is Alex Dalyac's, co-founder of unicorn Tractable, Edge Stack Rank:

Edge Stack Rank: Alex, CEO Tractable

PRIMARY

CATALYST

- Strong commerciality.
- Exposure to multiple markets and countries.
- Basic software development skills.

SECONDARY

TECH EDGE

- He had a Computer Science conversion degree from Imperial College.
- He became obsessed with deep learning, which was novel and cutting edge in 2014.

TERTIARY

MARKET EDGE

- He had worked in fashion at Lazada and tried to build his own fashion company.
- He also had exposure to the pipe welding market through his masters (which became the first use case for Tractable).

Chapter Summary

Defining your specific, personal, competitive advantage – your Edge – is a prerequisite for generating a strong idea with a compatible co-founder because:

- Past behaviour is the best predictor of future behaviour. Understand what you've done in the past and how it can contribute to your success as a founder.
- Assessing the experience, skills and behaviours that give you your Edge brings clarity to conversations with potential co-founders.
- Deep industry knowledge isn't as important as a willingness to challenge the status quo.

CHAPTER 7

How to Use Your Edge

The Power of Unique Edge Intersections

Great founders are usually exceptional, but they're rarely the best in the world in a single dimension. More often, they're very – but not necessarily *extraordinarily* – good in multiple complementary domains.

Let's say you are in the top 10 per cent in Skill 1 and in the top 10 per cent in Skill 2. Assuming those skills are reasonably uncorrelated, that puts you in the top 1 per cent (0.1*0.1) of people for that *combined* skill set.[12] It can be a particular sweet spot when one or more of your highly developed skills is uncommon for people in your industry. For example, if Skill 1 is knowledge of medicine and Skill 2 is commerciality, you should explore startup ideas that allow you to maximize this combined advantage. Take the time to look at your answers to each of the questions we posed in Chapter 6. Revisit your Edge stack rank. Where are there interesting, unique intersections?

Take Srinidhi Moodalagiri, co-founder of Flippy. He mined his first bitcoin at age sixteen, and after he graduated, he joined American Express for two years. When we worked with him, he realized that he had a powerful and unique intersection between his knowledge of Gen Z, cryptocurrencies and the world of professional finance. 'Gen Z struggles to understand crypto and struggles even more to invest into it. This is where I knew I could add the most value and create the most impact.' He channelled his ambition and deep knowledge of blockchain to build the first-of-its-kind crypto platform for Gen Z in India.

---

[12] 'How To Build An Edge: Develop Your Talent Stack - Personal Excellence.' Accessed November 19, 2021. https://personalexcellence.co/blog/talent-stack/.

Edge Stack Rank is like having a set
of playing cards in your hand

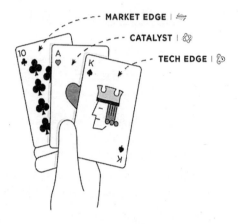

Let's recall the imagery of having a collection of Edges – a hand of cards you could play. You need to know the cards in your hand, the strength of those cards in relation to each other, and how they can intersect together. As you go through your co-founder and ideation conversations (both of which we'll explain in the next two chapters), you'll test out which of those cards you want to play. And since co-founding is about playing to the strengths of the team, you're looking at how to maximize the value of the intersection between your cards and those of your co-founder.

Comparing your cards
with your co-founder

Maximizing your Chances of Success with Edge

Let's revisit Tractable, the company we ended the previous chapter with. The Tractable co-founders, Alex Dalyac and Razvan Ranca, used their Edges to form their team and as the foundation for their idea. Razvan had a strong Tech Edge, having studied for a research masters with one of the top machine-learning professors in the world. Alex had a slightly more complicated background. He was a Catalyst, honed by his time at Rocket Internet in Asia – but his conversion degree in computer science gave him the basis of a Tech Edge, too, given that he became obsessed with the emerging field of deep learning. By itself, it wasn't enough to build a world-leading AI company, but it did mean he knew enough to see how the technology would change the world. It also gave him enough technical credibility to convince Razvan to work with him. Tractable is a unicorn today, but it only got started because Alex and Razvan recognized each other's unique strengths and that they were collectively more than the sum of their parts.

Edge makes ideas strong

Edge means you're more likely to get to founder-idea fit. Building a company is fraught with uncertainty and unknowns. There are many things that you can't control which may cause you to fail. One thing that *is* in your control is working on a problem that you understand and find endlessly fascinating. How you have spent your time over your career or academic life is usually a good indicator of the areas you should explore as a startup founder. Ultimately, your goal is to iterate an idea to find product-market fit. Working from your Edge gets you to that point quickly because your foundational elements (network, knowledge) are already established.

Edge increases your velocity of learning. As a founder, you are developing hunches about the problem you're solving and how this translates into a solution. You are constantly talking to customers and gathering feedback. To move fast, you need to be able to distinguish signal from noise. By using your Edge and your co-founder's Edge, you're more likely to have intuition about the problem you're solving. You have the insight to make fast decisions based on imperfect information. The best founders use their unfair advantage to iterate in an unexpected way. They see powerful pivots where others would just go back to the drawing board.

Edge creates differentiated ideas. Just because you've experienced a problem before doesn't mean you are the best person to solve it. Founders need to understand the landscape of obvious solutions (and why they failed) before they can find the non-obvious one (and why now is the time for it). Using your Edge will help you do this.

Edge-based ideas make fundraising easier. There are two important questions almost every investor will ask you: 'Why you?' and 'Why now?' Edge helps you answer both. Using your Edge gives you an easy way to articulate your advantage in solving a problem relative to other founders in the space. You have the skills and expertise that indicate you can outperform. You understand why the problem is ripe to solve now. You will have existing knowledge about the market, technology or regulatory changes and why *now* is the right time for this idea.

Edge makes teams strong

Edge accelerates the team-building process, which we'll cover in Chapter 9. By sharing your Edges with a potential co-founder, you can quickly understand each other's areas of expertise and then determine whether it's worth experimenting as a co-founding team.

You can combine Edges to maximize your chance of success. Edge helps co-founding teams quickly identify unusual and unique intersections in skills and experience. What might be most valuable is your unique combination of Edges rather than one standalone

Edge. These intersections enable you to build a category-defining company rather than one that gets stuck in a hyper-competitive space, trying to steal market share. You're innovating in emerging domains with massive market potential, such as enterprise conversational intelligence, instead of wading into the pool of dating or dining delivery apps. Category-defining companies often see their brand name or action evolve into a verb: 'Let's Uber to the party,' or 'We met when she swiped right.'

You can clearly see the opportunity cost of partnering with the wrong co-founder. The team you are forming should engage your greatest strengths. Understanding your Edge enables you to make an early exit from a team where there's no real competitive advantage. It allows you to focus on building a company with someone whose Edge, when combined with yours, offers world-changing potential.

You look at yourself more objectively. When founders search for their ideal partner using Edge, they naturally focus on finding someone who is a good fit *for them*. But great co-founding teams need to work for both founders. Developing deep knowledge of your own strengths helps you think clearly about whether you're also a good fit for your partner.

Getting Feedback

If you're not sure what your Edge is, test it by talking with people in your network. At EF, we often have one-on-one meetings with founders to walk through their background, skills and experience. We find that a lot of people undervalue what is most distinctive about them. They tend to gravitate towards things that are quite generic. Sometimes, people have an investment in their personal brand that doesn't necessarily correlate with their true Edge, or they want to 'get away' from their day job when they found a company.

Finding your Edge requires confidence and assertiveness, specifically around naming what you're great at while also being realistic about your weaknesses – both of which can make you feel vulnerable. In exploring your Edge, it can be helpful to have a conversation with a colleague, mentor or coach who can give you real – and sometimes tough to hear – feedback on your strengths and development areas.

You want to be very honest about where your advantage lies. Is there an industry in which you have a Market Edge? Is it truly an Edge or just a hobby? (Lots of people initially think they have a Market Edge in music or sport. For it to be an Edge, you need a genuinely distinctive insight about a space, not just a love for it.) If you think you might have a Technical Edge, try to be precise about what it is you know how to do that other founders might not. If you have a Catalyst Edge, solicit feedback on how distinctive your track record and behaviours really are.

Right to Win

You may have multiple strengths, but you should lean into your *primary* Edge. Your primary Edge could take the form of your most valuable, highly developed technical skill or your deepest area of expertise. If we think of your Edge as a hand of cards, your primary Edge is your strongest card. You should have evidence for your primary Edge. Edge gives you the right to win with the right idea.

Most people overrate the uniqueness of any one idea. We see thousands of applications to EF, and it's striking how within any cohort, themes emerge. It's like the idea's time has come, and suddenly there's not just one person talking about it but dozens – each of whom believe it's unique and special to them. Most good ideas are tried by multiple people simultaneously.

It's not enough to have the idea whose time has come. You need to be the right person for the idea. We call this founder-idea fit. When we talk about your 'right to win', we are referencing the unseen competition that's working on the same idea. Many founders make the mistake of thinking it's great to have no competition. But if no one else is doing what you're doing, it's usually a bad sign. It probably means it is a bad idea! Given this, one of the filters we use at EF is to ask: 'Let's assume that there are going to be a lot of people trying to do this – why will you win?'

What is it about you that will make your startup not just good but the best in the world at what it does? Our goal as investors is to back category winners – as we'll discuss later, it's hard to succeed in VC otherwise – and this means that we usually do not support ideas where the market will be highly fragmented with no single firm standing out. We're looking to fund companies that are going to dominate their space. And so, the founder's right to win is key.

This is a good mindset for founders, too. You are investing your time in your startup, and you don't get any of the diversification of risk that the VCs get when they invest their money. Even if you're not interested in seeking venture capital, if you're going to spend years working on this thing, you better believe you're going to be the winner.

We encourage founders to imagine six months ahead – the moment they are pitching their company for seed investment. We ask founders, 'What is the company that you can start such that when you stand on that stage and people hear the story of what you've done in the past, your background, your skills, your experience, they will say, "*Yes – obviously, this person should start this company*"?' That's your right to win.

You and your team will have a right to win if you have the combination of knowledge, skills, experience and network to tackle the right problem, create the right solution and build the right team. The best way to ensure you do is to lean into your Edge.

The Problem of Passion

We're wary of the word 'passion' at EF. Passion can lead you astray. We've seen too many founders dismiss their Edge because they're keen to work on their passions. The lawyer who wanted to build a beauty marketplace. The machine-learning PhD who wanted to build a product for football. There are exceptions – there always are in startups – but too often, this leads to undifferentiated insights and no right to win.

Edge is <u>not</u> passion. You can be passionate about many things, particularly hobbies. But it's unlikely you are a world-class expert in subjects such as music, sport or arts unless you've dedicated a significant amount of time pursuing them professionally. Keep playing guitar as a creative outlet, but don't focus your ideation energy on it.

Your Edge is an area that should sustain your interest and inspire you to keep learning. It should be compelling enough to you that you're excited to dedicate the next decade of your life to exploring it.

'Want to win' matters. Although passion doesn't equal edge, the strongest ideas will sit at the intersection of your 'right to win' (the thing you are uniquely positioned to do) and 'want to win' (the thing you're *excited* to build). Your 'right to win' will come from your primary edge – your strongest card – but remember, you have to *want* to play that card.

Sara Clemens, COO of Twitch and angel investor, said she sees this in the strongest founders she has worked with at companies like Pandora and Duolingo. 'Founders have an innate belief that something is broken and that they are the right person to fix it. Their desire to found a company is based on the belief that something can be made better and that they are uniquely suited to do that.'

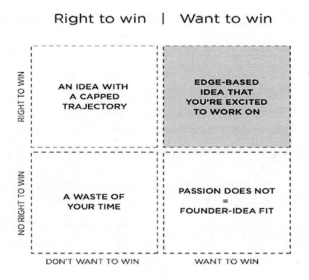

Right to win | Want to win

Don't Let Your Edge Put You in a Box

When we first introduce this idea to new entrepreneurs, they tend to hate Edge because it makes them feel as if they are being pigeonholed, and no one – especially a founder – likes being put in a box.

Edge is just a starting point – a framework, not an iron law. It's a way to sharpen your focus about what to work on and who to work with. It's about accelerating your journey as a founder by enabling you to find the right idea and co-founder for you. Using this framework successfully isn't about ticking every box. It's about using it as inspiration for what is inherently a very creative process. You will note that we have posed many questions to you during this chapter. The practice of answering these questions and the introspection this creates is the true value of this framework. Edge is a powerful starting point and way of thinking, not a step-by-step guidebook.

Being a founder is hard and high-risk. Edge is your secret weapon in building a globally important company. Edge will enable you to identify the problems **you** are best suited to solve. The smartest founders maximize their chances of success and reduce risk by identifying their

Edge and using edge-based ideation to build a co-founding team. That's what we turn to next.

Chapter Summary

Co-founding is about playing to the strengths of the team, and Edge helps you evaluate potential ideas.

- Edge – not passion, inspiration or market trends – should be the starting point for finding founder-idea fit.
- Edge allows you to maximize the value of the intersection between your greatest strengths and that of your co-founder.
- Use Edge to navigate early-stage compatibility and role definition in your team.
- Use Edge to frame your right to win for investors.

CHAPTER 8

Choosing Your Co-founder

You're having dinner with some of your friends, and you start talking about how much you'd like to found a startup. One friend gets excited and says they feel the same way and that they can't stand their boss. Over a few too many drinks, you look across the table at one another and think, *We're on to something.* You hash out ideas, and by the end of the night, you've both decided to quit your job and go all in. Six months later, you can't stand each other, and the idea has gone nowhere. The idea – not to mention the friendship – has fizzled out.

Or maybe you have what you think is a brilliant idea, and you know that you need someone with a technical background, so a friend connects you to the only engineer they know. You are unsure about them, but you don't want to waste too much time looking, so you're willing to take the risk. You spend weeks trying to convince them to buy into your vision and working out how you will split the equity in the company. You have a vague sense of unease, and it's difficult to put a voice to it, but you want to be a founder, so you are willing to settle.

A few months in, you already know the relationship isn't working. You can't imagine spending the next year working with them, let alone the next five to ten years. But because you're unsure and new at this, you put off thinking about it. In any event, you are hesitant to have the awkward conversation that would have to come before breaking up, so you avoid it.

Weeks go by, and then months, and now you've actually got a prototype and some early users, so you both feel possessive of the company. By the time the conversation happens, it's not so much a talk as it is a yelling match. You have a protracted negotiation over the (probably very limited) assets of the company. It's so draining that you throw your hands up and walk away from it all, leaving months (or maybe years) of work and effort behind you.

This is, alas, a typical co-founder 'love story' with an unhappy ending. Such stories are not talked about much, though occasionally they're immortalized in film, as in *The Social Network*. These breakups are emotionally and financially messy. What's more, the opportunity cost is real. The time you waste on the wrong idea and with the wrong co-founder delays your globally important idea. When first-time founders start a company, they tend to focus almost exclusively on getting the right idea and accepting a 'co-founder of convenience'. This is a mistake. While the initial idea is important, choosing the right co-founder is *far* more important. Quod AI founder Hervé Vũ Roussel said, 'I knew that picking the right co-founder was key to the success of this adventure. I had a high bar for my co-founder. I would have rather left with nothing than to start a company with someone that I didn't have great admiration for.'

Breakup messiness is a consequence of the limited pool of co-founders many aspiring entrepreneurs are choosing from, a lack of understanding of what a good co-founding partnership looks like, and a lack of guidance on the *practice* of building a successful co-founding relationship. We want to challenge the norm that the idea comes first. In our experience, you can't separate choosing the right idea from choosing the right co-founder – and getting both right in parallel is fundamental to startup success.

As we discussed in the chapter on Edge, Founder DNA dictates the DNA of business – what kind of ideas you should work on, what kind of markets you can win in, how fast you can move and whether you can raise funding. The right pairing can create truly differentiated, world-leading ideas. The team building and ideation processes feed off each other and can only work if both are aligned. Your idea and your team need to be developed and tested simultaneously.

New founders tend to treat the process as if they are looking for a new friend. As you'll be spending the majority of your waking hours together, it can be tempting to focus on whether you have shared interests or a sense of humour. But you're not looking for a friend; you're looking for, and hiring, a business partner.

It's helpful to think of finding a co-founder in the same way as making a hiring decision – albeit hiring an equal. This is a critical mindset shift we encourage from the beginning. If you believe your company will be successful, choosing your co-founder will also become the most significant financial decision of your life. Because half the ownership of your business is at stake, you must believe that your co-founder is at least going to double your chances of success or double the ultimate outcome for the business. Ideally, both you and your co-founder *each* believe that the other will more than double the value of your equity. A successful serial entrepreneur once put it to us that the perfect set-up is where each co-founder feels the other is a little bit better than themselves.

In this chapter, we'll teach you how to find the right co-founder for you and the business you want to create.

Two's Company?

Perhaps the most fundamental question is, how many co-founders do you need? There are some famous companies – like Amazon – with just one, others – like Airbnb – with three, and some with even more. We recommend that most people, though, start a company with one other person.

There are three important reasons:

1. Going it alone is an enormous emotional and practical burden. As Paul Graham, co-founder of Y Combinator, has said, 'a startup is too much work for one person'.

2. Having too many co-founders introduces too much relationship complexity. In a co-founding team of two, you have one interpersonal dynamic to manage. Adding an extra co-founder doesn't make it 50 per cent but three times more complex – there are now three dynamics to manage.

3. Having too many co-founders is expensive. Splitting equity three ways means a third less equity for you. If the skill set of the third co-founder could be provided by an early employee, you probably save thirty points of equity! (Early employees who receive a salary from the start usually get low single-digit percentages of equity.)

Understanding Roles

In the early days of the startup, before you've raised your funding or have any semblance of a product-market fit, founder roles might not be very distinct. At first, both of you should be deeply involved in customer and product development – and, early on, that's pretty much all you should be doing. Nevertheless, it's helpful to understand the roles you will eventually play so you can find a strong co-founder balance.

Every startup requires that certain activities get done, ideally by someone who gets satisfaction from doing them. Rather than getting hung up on titles like CEO (Chief Executive Officer), CTO (Chief Technology Officer) or COO (Chief Operating Officer), we recommend looking at the required skill sets of each position and identify whether you have the ability – and the willingness – to succeed in that role.

Willingness is an overlooked element. Being a founder is a difficult career path that doesn't get much easier with time. Elad Gil, tech exec, angel investor and author of the *High Growth Handbook*, said, 'A common trigger of founder burnout is finding yourself working on things that you hate.' If you end up in a role that doesn't fit your preferences and abilities, it's unlikely that you'll succeed in that role for the long term.

It can be easy to push the 'roles conversation' further down the line, especially if you're nervous about how it will go. We encourage you to have this conversation upfront. Even if it's a moment of potential conflict, this is a great test for how you negotiate and make decisions together. Remember, the easiest time to resolve fundamental questions about your roles is before your company is valuable enough to matter. If you've always had clarity, it is much less likely that these things become contentious down the line. Incentives and emotions change once there's more at stake.

Eventually, the day-to-day work will become more aligned with specific roles. As co-founders, you are probably hiring yourselves into your company's first 'C-level' roles, so it's important to talk honestly about who has the best chance of being world-class in each role. Of course, if there's not a role that you or your co-founder can be exceptional at, this isn't the right company for you – and, even if painful, it's good to discover that as soon as possible.

CEO

Every startup needs a CEO. This is often a role that leads to contentious conversations. It appears to be the most important position. But being CEO is not just about a fancy title; it's a very specific role that suits some personalities and skill sets better than others. Your CEO is your primary salesperson. It's critical they not only connect comfortably with a variety of audiences but can close a deal. Your company's ability to fundraise, find and understand customers, negotiate partnerships and lure top talent hinges on your CEO's persuasive powers.

If you want to build a high-growth company, you will likely need to be fuelled by venture capital. Many of the founders we work with are surprised to learn how much of the CEO's time is spent fundraising (potentially six months out of every eighteen!). Many of our best CEOs are those who enjoy the process of raising capital and don't shy away from pitching. Fundraising involves spending a lot of time with people, networking and attending events to get your face in front of potential investors. Good CEOs can take the consistent stream of no's from potential investors and persuade those who are interested to get over the line.

'A great market or a great idea is worthless without truly exceptional founders,' said London-based entrepreneur and angel investor Chris Mairs, who founded Sequoia-backed Metaswitch, which was acquired by Microsoft. 'This particularly applies to the CEO. I identify this, in a very intuitive way, through their constant ability to surprise and delight. They need to weave a compelling narrative, backed up by evidence, and based on insights which are on the one hand surprising but on the other hand delightfully obvious once explained.'

Alongside fundraising, the CEO is normally in charge of thinking about how the startup will make money. The best CEOs are commercially minded. They enjoy thinking about the creation of their business model and how they can optimize it over time. The business model is an articulation of how the company will create value for their user and capture some of that value to generate profits.

World-class startup CEOs can think macro and micro simultaneously. They can hold in their head the vision for where the company is going and connect that vision to what the team is doing that day. The best CEOs then communicate this effectively to their team and investors.

If you have strong Market and Catalyst Edges, it's more likely that you are going to take on the CEO role. However, it's worth noting that many of the strongest CEOs in our portfolio have secondary Tech Edges, as do Mark Zuckerberg (Facebook), Anne Wojcicki (23andMe) and Sachin Bansal (Flipkart). Remember, it's about will and skill. You need to be both willing to do the role and prepared to develop the skill to excel in it.

CTO/COO

Particularly pre-seed, the primary responsibility of the CTO is to be a founder. Nevertheless, there always needs to be at least one person on the founding team who can build and ship the product's first version. If you are building a technology company, we would strongly recommend having a CTO on the founding team, but do not settle for working with the only Tech Edge in your network just because they provide that critical skill you lack. Too often, we see co-founders compromise on a strong match in this area because they don't believe they have many options. We'll cover the options they actually have later on.

If you're doing something operationally or logistically intensive, however, then a COO might be a role you need to fill on the founding team. COOs tend to be the 'fixers' and the doers. Specific CTO and COO responsibilities may differ drastically depending on the nature of the industry in which you are founding, but you can expect to be focused on work that continually drives the product forward.

A common error we see co-founders make is double-CEO or double-CTO teams. They're usually a 'co-founder of convenience' situation – you knew each other and wanted to start a company at the same time. You possibly didn't consider how you would intersect as co-founders or understand what enables you to create (and prevents you from creating).

If you've got two CEOs, you're likely to generate energy around big ideas. You're out talking to everyone and may even be able to raise lots of money. But building – turning ideas into a product that functions – becomes an issue. With two CTOs, you're very likely to concentrate on the opposite direction. You're too focused on the technical side of building the product without having key conversations with customers and investors. This can lead to a short-lived idea, and you won't have a well-developed business model or funding to grow.

There are counterexamples to this, but generally, a lack of heterogeneity in the co-founding team calls for examination. Do you really think this is the best co-founder combination for you? Or is it what you've settled on due to lack of options?

What to Look for in a Co-founder

Many fledgling founders struggle to know what to look for in a co-founder. They might have been too influenced by typical founder stereotypes in the media and have a set view of what they want. They might have a strongly held idea and want someone to build it for them. However, having a very strong ongoing hypothesis of what you're looking for narrows your search parameters and shuts you off from the full set of co-founding opportunities you might have.

Ultimately, you're trying to find a business partner. Someone who you will work alongside for many years – not someone who you will work for, and not someone who will work for you. It's one of the closest relationships you will have in your life, and you will spend more waking hours with them than anyone else. You're looking for someone who ultimately energizes you, makes you super productive, inspires you to be the best version of yourself and shares the same beliefs about what you want to create. The best co-founders share a deep respect for the other person and what they bring to the table. Both should feel lucky to work with each other.

When we select individuals at EF, we want to know about their past behaviour. Past behaviour is the strongest and most reliable indicator of how someone will behave in the future. We have seen this time and again at EF. Even if someone says they're entrepreneurial, if they haven't demonstrated some key behaviours before founding (exemplified by the criteria we outlined in Part 1, Chapter 4), it's unlikely they're going to change their spots overnight. We encourage you to take the same approach when screening potential co-founders.

When you start meeting potential co-founders, have our criteria in your back pocket. You should understand which of these traits you have and which of these traits a potential co-founder might have. Ask them lots of questions to fully understand what they've done in the past and how that might feed into their Edge. Understand their Edges, and don't be afraid to ask for 'proof' i.e., examples to show the depth of their knowledge, skills and behaviours.

When finding a co-founder, it can be tempting to find someone who is similar to you or the polar opposite to you. Neither of these approaches is quite right. You want a balance of the two. Co-founding teams who are identical in skills and experience can struggle to have the balance required to bring the company to life. On the flip side, co-founding teams with no commonality can find it hard to be productive as there is no shared language, experience or working style. The ideal co-founding team has a degree of overlap. This is where the Edge framework can be helpful. By understanding each other's Edge stack rank, you can identify where you might have overlap.

We have seen that teams with different Edge combinations outperform those with the same primary Edge. There are exceptions, but the highest performing teams typically have two different primary Edges on the co-founding team. Magic Pony Technology – a London-based machine learning startup that was bought by Twitter eighteen months after it was founded for a reported $150m – had a well-balanced founding team. Rob Bishop's (CEO) primary Catalyst Edge meant he leant into creating a route to market for the product and fundraising. His secondary Tech Edge from his electronic engineering degree meant he had a shared understanding with his CTO, Zehan Wang. Zehan had a Primary Tech Edge from his PhD in computer vision.

How to Find a Potential Partner

We find people lower the bar for their co-founders in a way that they wouldn't for somebody they hire, largely because of the limited options. At Entrepreneur First, we solved this problem by bringing together carefully screened groups of potential founders to create optionality. Outside of EF, you're much more likely to have a less diverse and smaller network of potential co-founders, most of whom are very similar to you. That homogeneity constrains the ideas that you can end up working on. If you don't have a specific edge, building certain ideas will be very difficult. Because of this lack of available alternatives, the average new founder compromises and ends up co-founding with somebody who isn't – or doesn't have the opportunity to be – a world-class version of a CEO or CTO. As you go through the co-founder search process, you need to ask yourself, 'Is this the best possible co-founder I can find, or is this the most convenient co-founder I can find?'

The first step to finding a co-founder is understanding yourself as discussed in the previous chapters. By digging into your Edges, stack ranking them and looking at the unique intersections, you are preparing yourself for effective co-founder conversations.

Next, you need to understand your options – those that already exist and those that you need to manufacture. You are looking to unearth an exceptional co-founder. This will take time and conscious, strategic effort. It's the most important decision you will make when founding your startup – and one that is consistently undervalued by first-time founders. There are two ways to think about your available network of co-founders: those who are currently in your network and those who could be in the future.

Who you currently know

New founders often think the ideal is to find a co-founder among people with whom you already have a relationship. In our experience, these co-founding relationships have very stark outcomes. They can be incredibly powerful when two individuals know how the other works, their quirks and their history. This can enable them to be quickly and enduringly productive. However, it's not a slam dunk. We have seen many of these friendship-based co-founding relationships end messily and emotionally. When you have known someone for years, you're less selective and struggle to accurately evaluate the other person's skills. You often shy away from tough feedback, allowing resentment to build.

The key point here is that you don't *need* to have a long-standing relationship with a potential co-founder. This shouldn't be a limiting factor when you consider building a startup. Take the time to understand and examine who is in your network already. Scope out the different people you have met during your life – it can be helpful to map them out against the different Edge categories.

The co-founding story behind 23andMe follows this pattern. Co-founders Anne Wojcicki and Linda Avey had known of each other for a while, but it wasn't until Linda invited Anne to an industry dinner that they established a relationship. They then kept bumping into each other by being in the same biotech circles. It wasn't until they were both at the same TED conference that Anne started asking Linda tonnes of questions about her fledgling idea. 'Right before we jumped into our cars to drive home, she told me she wanted to "do" this new company with me,' Linda said, and 23andMe was born. Anne and Linda are an example of a strong Edge intersection. Linda had a primary Tech Edge with a background in biology. Anne had a Market Edge from working as a healthcare investment analyst.

Even if you are early in your career, it's likely your network is much larger than you think. Your friends, extended family, colleagues from internships and loose connections from university are all in your network. A network is not something you get from networking; it's something you build every time you interact with someone (whether in a personal or professional context). You often meet a co-founder through an introduction from someone in your network, someone who is one degree away. Ensure your network knows that you're looking and be clear and specific about what you're looking for – skills and readiness to found.

Erica Young, Head of Community and Network for the venture capital firm Anthemis and founder of The Reliants Project, applies her expertise around networks to support the growth of portfolio companies. In her experience, entrepreneurial appetite is a key filter for narrowing the field. When you start a conversation with a potential co-founder by introducing the problem you are seeking to solve, they may get excited about exploring ideas but baulk at taking the leap. So often, potential co-founders get far into the conversation, and then one drops out because the reality of what they're about to undertake finally hits them. For that reason, Young recommends that these exploratory conversations begin by discussing Edges *and* the desire to be a founder.

Filtering for readiness to found can be difficult, but listen for the cues they'll give you in their speech. Some will be direct about their interest level. Other indirect cues can be a red flag. When they talk, listen to how they frame themselves in their life circumstances. Do they victimize themselves and rely on excuses or do they articulate with clarity and confidence how they are creating their life? If it's the former, you're better off continuing your search. As Young puts it, the single biggest signal that they're not ready to found is if they tell you they're 'weighing their options' or that they're thinking of starting a company but also applied for a job – and an MBA programme. Someone with deep entrepreneurial desires isn't interested in other options.

Who you could know

Networks are live and evolving things that, with strategic effort, can grow reasonably quickly. Young advises that when you start looking for a potential co-founder, remember that like hangs out with like. Founders hang out with other founders. Domain experts in a particular area probably know a lot of other domain experts. People who care about a particular problem seek out others who share their concerns and interests. So, if you decide you need to meet someone with a particular skill set, start there – think about who you know that has that skill set, and then ask them for help in finding others like them. If you look around and realize you know no one who fits that description, then you need to proactively embed yourself in a related network.

As for finding these people, there are so many entry points that it's easy to get started. Online options abound. There are Slack communities, WhatsApp groups, Telegram threads, Discord conversations that are organized by thought leaders in every given domain. The more niche you can get in your search, the better. Brian Armstrong, co-founder of Coinbase, went to a Bitcoin subreddit and Hacker News to find a co-founder. 'You must be technical, have a passion for this space, and have insane work ethic. This is going to be super f***ing hard, but the payoff is that we have a non-zero chance of really changing the world in a big way. This isn't another photo sharing app.' He posted this on Hacker News and soon met Fred Ersham. Together they built the world's largest cryptocurrency exchange platform.

Like Brian Armstrong, you're better off going to a narrow online group or in-person event than showing up at a conference with thousands of attendees hoping to make a connection. Co-founders of ClassDojo Sam Chaudhary and Liam Don met at a hack weekend in Cambridge, UK. They met up for coffee the week after the event and discovered that they were both extremely passionate about fixing education at scale. They had each been working on ideas already and decided to work together. Just a few weeks later, Sam quit his job and Liam put his PhD on hold, and they moved to Silicon Valley. Just a brief connection at a conference led them to build one of the most successful ed-tech companies in the US, with 95 per cent of early years schools using the platform.

Finally, when possible, get specific about asking for introductions. For example, when you enter an online community, introduce yourself to the person who set up that community. Then tell them that you're interested in XYZ, and you'd like to know three to five people you should meet who are into the same topic matter. You've given them enough context, and you've been specific, which makes it easier for them. This worked for Hopin co-founder Dave Schools. He met Johnny Boufarhat while 'interviewing the super-connector founder of a very large Slack community for an article and he fired off a number of quick one-line email introductions. One of them was to Johnny.' They built a remote co-founding relationship that underpinned Hopin's meteoric rise to a $5bn+ valuation in just two years.

Building a network takes time, but if you're focused, you should make some good headway within a matter of months. Remember, relationships take time to build, and so will your search for the right co-founder. It takes careful listening to understand a particular community and the people within it. If you feel tension around the idea of intentionally building your network because you don't want to come off as aggressive, insincere or opportunistic in your search, shift from a 'calculated' to a 'cultivated' approach. Be sure to thank people who open doors, and keep in touch when you see opportunities that align with the interests of those who have helped you along the way. By cultivating your network, you're not leaving your startup or your network to chance.

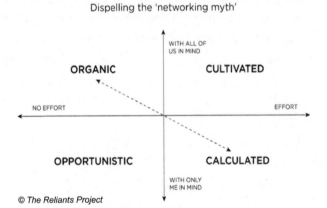

Dispelling the 'networking myth'

© The Reliants Project

Ultimately, when you connect with the right co-founder – whether it's working with someone you've known since primary school or a technologist you met through six degrees of Slack – your startup story begins. Your co-founding team is the foundation of your startup and by investing in this upfront you are giving yourself the best chance of success.

Chapter Summary

Edge emphasizes strategy over serendipity in finding the right co-founder.

- Don't settle for a co-founder of convenience. This could be one of the most important relationships in your life and you should invest accordingly in finding the right co-founder.
- A co-founder is a business partner first and a friend second.
- Even though co-founders share similar responsibilities in the early stages of a startup, defining roles from the outset prevents future friction.
- Actively and deliberately cultivating your network will improve your chances of connecting with a world-class co-founder.

CHAPTER 9

Working with Your Co-founder and Testing the Team

When thinking about testing a co-founder relationship, many founders default to talking. They want to talk about ideas together, shared interests or how their values align. Although this can be a good way to get to know someone, it doesn't help you understand whether you can work together. Ultimately, a co-founder relationship is a *working* relationship. This means the most important thing to test is how you work together.

From our experience, the best way to evaluate whether your co-founder is the right one is to see how productive you are together. It's easy to do work that keeps you busy but means nothing. It's easy to get overly focused on the process and lose sight of your outcomes and achievements (or lack thereof). Our mantra is '**productivity is traction for teams**'. Once you have a product and customers, traction is measured in metrics. Before that, in the early days of a startup, traction is measured in learning. Rob Bishop, exited founder of Magic Pony Technology, said, 'A great founder and team take pride in the pace at which they can learn, not necessarily pride in the correctness of their intuition or the fact that their original idea was proved correct.'

The best teams are those that can generate significant learning very quickly. They test a different hypothesis each week. In the very early stages of a startup, you don't necessarily want to be building – you want to be talking to people who enable you to update your hypotheses. *As a team, can you synthesize deep, interesting insights that progress your knowledge of the market quickly?* Not only does this process enable you to test and develop your idea, but it also helps to evaluate the co-founding relationship. Think about the information-gathering process across two dimensions – information on how your idea should develop and evolve, and information on whether you should continue with this co-founder.

Most people have a reasonably intuitive sense of whether they are being productive. We know what it feels like to be operating at our peak performance. Successful co-founding teams talk about their shared learning process as happening faster than they thought was possible. Somehow, their joint productivity exceeds the sum of the parts. The best co-founding teams talk about how speed became natural. On the flipside, in poor-performing teams, co-founders settle for their joint productivity falling below their personal capabilities. We push teams early on to make breakups almost the default, so they don't waste time in a pairing that can't be productive.

At EF, we can put a price on the productivity of the best teams we've worked with. It's not unusual for our top performing teams to generate $1m of value every week they work together. We measure this retrospectively by dividing their latest raise valuation by the number of weeks they've been working together. If you believe you could be a globally important founder, you should recognize the potential $1m+ weekly opportunity cost of being in the wrong team.

Ideally, you have chosen a co-founder who has a distinct circle of competence. They trust themselves, and you trust them to make the right call. It requires both confidence in their ability and some humility to admit what decisions lie outside of their circle of competence. Don't let those circles become silos. Check in with each other every day. Problem-solve together. Even as you acknowledge distinct areas of expertise, don't carve up work so that one of you is talking to customers and one of you is coding. We often see co-founders going in quite different directions very early on, with one covering customer development and the other focusing on product development. As a result, they don't spend enough time together. This means even if the idea is progressing, they aren't testing out their co-founding relationship. Remember: you're still testing the team.

If you're having intense conversations about beliefs and equity, it can be tempting to leave unspoken more fundamental topics such as motivation, work and communication style and ethics. Beyond getting to know their big ideas and beliefs, you should have a sense of their personal preferences, life story and values. We have seen founders use the now-famous '36 Questions to Bring You Closer Together' by Dr Arthur Aron. Designed to foster intimacy in under an hour, these questions are a helpful shortcut for co-founders who want to get well-acquainted quickly. You can find links to this and other tools to understand each other at howtobeafounder.com.

Early-stage founders understand that you have to talk to customers, but often they will learn something from their customers and forget to bring it back to the co-founder. At this stage, you are constantly co-creating the foundations of the company. You should be approaching people for customer development together (more on this in Chapter 11). Spend time debriefing with your co-founder and looking for themes and patterns that allow you to update your hypothesis, test your learning and help build your co-founder relationship. Co-founders that are functioning well are excited to share their new discoveries with each other.

Testing your team/productivity should be done directly and regularly. We encourage teams to institute a daily stand-up meeting where both co-founders answer a consistent set of questions at the end of each day. The core questions are:

1. **What do we know now that we didn't know this morning?** This ensures teams test productivity on what they learn (i.e., an insight from customer development), not just what they've done (i.e., number of customer development calls). If you don't have a good answer to this question – if you're not learning – how productive have you truly been?

2. **On a scale of 1–10, excluding 7, how happy do you feel in this team?** This takes a potentially awkward and emotional question and makes it feel factual and objective. By eliminating the 'safe' choice of seven, you have to take an authentic look at your feelings. If you ask this question of yourselves every day, there is much less friction if you say '2' than if you had to bring it up in a conversation out of the blue. It's also an opportunity to differentiate between the traction you're experiencing externally and any internal team turmoil. If you are getting loads of customer interest, it's easy to gloss over co-founder doubts.

The idea behind the daily meeting is that you want to close the gap between intention and effect – particularly if you're working with someone you don't actually know that well. We've found that tension in a team can come as a result of small miscommunications. These arise because two co-founders aren't familiar with the way the other interacts – there's a gap between what one person intended and what the other heard. Daily feedback means these miscommunications can be spotted early on, and often ironed out. Having a formalized meeting each day allows you to quickly catch anomalies as they appear, which ensures that issues won't unnecessarily spiral. This also helps you more quickly identify what isn't working. Remember – the best founders will get into and out of co-founding teams fast.

One of the most important things you can learn to do is have radically honest conversations with your co-founder. 'The best thing you can do is deal with the conflict quickly. Discuss what you think about how the other works, any issues you have with their style or personality and what you can each do differently,' said Toby Mather, co-founder of ed-tech startup Lingumi.

The daily stand-up is a way to prioritize and ritualize this sense of honesty and urgency. A co-founding partnership is about business, but it is a human relationship that requires care and maintenance.

In a startup, there will be ups and downs. Issues don't just 'sort themselves out' down the line. They only get bigger and harder to face. If you build up a well of resentment over issues that frustrate you, it can fundamentally undermine the potential success of the company. Early doubts resurface during growth periods when they're even more catastrophic for the business. Disharmony among co-founders is one of the most common reasons startups fail. Front-load relationships with discussions about things that really matter, such as conflicts in working styles or loss of belief in your idea.

The stand-up is also an opportunity to practise giving and receiving feedback, an essential skill as you grow your team. You don't want to have to learn to give and receive feedback when you're going through a crisis. By following a preferred feedback framework (like the OEPS Method, SKS Method or Stanford Method), founders can – and should – come to see feedback as a gift. A useful book on this is *Fierce Conversations* by Susan Scott, which provides a range of methods to have some of the more contentious discussions that arise between co-founders. You can read more about how to give feedback at howtobeafounder.com.

When you work for a large organization, there are mechanisms to address your professional development – performance reviews, peer appraisals, 360-degree feedback. When you are just a two-person team, none of these is readily available. You are simultaneously each other's boss, peer and subordinate. This means both giving and soliciting feedback graciously. Keep an open mindset and remain committed to change and growth. For the success of your company, you have an obligation to help each other to be the best possible leaders within the startup you are building.

No-stigma Breakups

There is no perfect formula for co-founder chemistry. Knowing you haven't found the right co-founder is part gut instinct and part paying attention to your productivity levels and ability to iterate together around an idea.

Founders typically avoid the break-up conversation for far too long. Some mismatches are obvious within hours. Others could work together relatively well for weeks without ever generating the spark of shared enthusiasm for exploring their hunches. You might cycle through multiple false starts before finally connecting with a strong match. We've taken steps to de-stigmatize breakups within our cohorts. Our teams enter a conversation assuming an early breakup is the default, not a failing. We even celebrate co-founder breakups at EF. When founders break up at EF, they get applauded by their peers for making the right call. Breakups get posted on our internal Slack channels and are covered in emoji celebrations. One of the nicest parts about this is that individual founders often try to 'sell on' their co-founder – although they weren't the right fit for each other, they explain their strengths and recommend them to someone else.

Breaking up with a co-founder or agreeing to move on from a partnership that isn't working can be fraught with emotion. You want to try to reduce the emotional impact of a breakup. By reducing the transaction costs of getting out of the partnerships, you are more likely to make the tough decision. Take the time to set up a clear testing period where you are both clear on what you're trying to achieve and the evaluation points along the way. Remember, the longer you stretch out an unproductive partnership, the more opportunities you and your partner miss. You want to make it as easy as possible to move on quickly. One helpful frame to remember is that if you don't think it's working, the worst thing you can do for the other person is keep going and pretend that everything is OK. You're not just wasting your time; you're wasting their time. It's your responsibility to make the conversation happen.

Watch for the red flags we discussed earlier: if you can't find a shared vision and have fierce conversations about the future of your business, it's time to part ways. When ending a co-founding relationship, focus the conversation on where the partnership isn't tracking against your goals, and stay away from assigning blame. If you've been using the daily stand-up formula we suggested previously, it's likely clear to both of you that something isn't working. If you've been working on an idea together, be clear about whether one of you plans to carry it forward.

It's also fine if both of you want to take the idea forward. At this very early stage, we have seen many co-founders break up and continue the idea in different directions to great success. If you're breaking up before a seed round, the idea is still just a starting point, and each founder will morph the idea based on their own and new co-founder's Edge. The customer development you will do will inevitably pull you in different directions, and the likelihood of competition is a lot lower than you might think.

As tempting as it can be, you cannot analytically decide whether you are the right co-founding pair. You can only decide by trying. How do you know when you're with The One? Try to work on something together and see how it feels. If you aren't able to find an idea together, or the iterative process isn't flowing, move on. Our advice: have a low bar for getting started and a high standard for staying together.

> *If you have 'founder envy,' where you look at another team and feel envious of their partnership, it means you're in the wrong team.*
> *Break up immediately.*
> Emilia Molimpakis, co-founder Thymia, London

Making the Partnership Official

You've done enough testing to know you plan to work together long-term. Now what? While specific legal elements of establishing your company will vary from country to country, three core principles remain universally important.

First, establish the equity split from the beginning. We recommend an equal split of ownership for co-founding teams where you're starting from scratch. In a startup, you're assuming that almost all the value of that equity will be created in the future. On Day One, the shares are worth zero. Value is created by what you do together. If you're joining a business that already exists, or if you're exploiting the previous work of one co-founder, you might reach a different agreement, but the principle here is that equity is forward-looking. It's not based on intellectual property created in the past.

Imagine you agree to a 60/40 split today. Fast forward ten years and the company is worth a billion dollars. Do you really feel that the difference in what you started with was worth $200 million after working side-by-side for ten years? Almost certainly not. Everything that happened prior to the birth of the company is essentially a rounding error compared to the amount of value that you'll create together if you succeed. This is why we recommend a 50/50 split. If you create a situation where one person resents that they own 20 per cent less or 15 per cent less of the company than the other person, even though they've been there for 99 per cent of the company's life relative to the other person, you're eventually going to be in a situation where that resentment poses more problems than having had an equal split from the start.

Split also factors into operations and governance. We're often asked who gets to make the final decision in a co-founder relationship. If ownership of the company is split equally, how do you settle disputes when there's no ultimate leader? We've been fortunate to be involved in over 300 companies, and we've never seen a company that makes voting decisions based on the number of shares each person holds. This is why it's important to separate how the company operates versus how the company governs. People overestimate the importance of voting and underestimate the importance of influence. The most existential decisions (e.g., whether to sell the business) should be taken genuinely with equal weight to the views and aspirations of both founders, assuming an equal equity split, which I usually advocate,' said investor Chris Mairs.

Even if the equity split was uneven, the person holding the higher share would get nowhere by using their larger share to trump the other person. That kind of power move builds resentment between co-founders, and resentment can kill a partnership. If you want to have a healthy partnership, it's best to have an equal split from the start, and discuss early on how you will make decisions when there is a difference of opinion. Chris Mairs said, 'At the day-to-day level, while the CEO needs to seek consensus from the other founder – and indeed from all stakeholders – the non-CEO founder equally needs to give the CEO the freedom to execute efficiently.' In the startup sphere, the latitude to make a quick decision is important. The majority of business decisions are matters of judgement – if you make the wrong choice, you can fix it later. When it comes to the organization of company ownership, however, a lack of clear agreement leads to equally unclear lines of authority and communication. This breeds dysfunction, which in turn may cause you to lose the competitive race.

Next, establish a legal agreement with your partner. Think of this step, taken after the initial testing period when you have started creating a product and seeing initial traction, as a marriage prenup. Navigating the path to legalized partnership is a great way to test having difficult conversations with your co-founder and to see how you negotiate with each other and make decisions together. It's not a sign of distrust to say that you need a legal agreement governing your relationship; it's a sign of professionalism. You're about to create an entity together that could become valuable.

With a contract in place from early on, you have a road map for difficult decisions that may come into play later. A written agreement about how the company is governed and how proceeds will be divided provides protection. And it's much easier to make these agreements when your company is worth nothing versus millions. If you're curious to see a template legal agreement, we have one on our book website at howtobeafounder.com.

Third, do not underestimate the importance of vesting. Many of the problems founders worry about with equal equity split are resolved by having a good vesting schedule. Vesting is the idea that if someone leaves the company before a certain period of time elapses, they forfeit a portion of their shares. If all the company's value is created in the future, you want to avoid a situation where if one co-founder quits after a month, they still own half the company at year ten.

Having a vesting schedule is the common best practice around the world. A conventional schedule dictates that a founder must work for four years to get 100 per cent of their shares. If they leave within the first year, they typically get nothing. After twelve months, you hit the 'cliff' and 'vest' 25 per cent. This means that if you leave the day after your first anniversary, you would keep a quarter of the shares you started with. After that, your shares vest in equal monthly instalments until you reach 100 per cent of your shares vested at the end of the fourth year. If you leave after that, you keep everything you started with. This schedule – 'four years with a one-year cliff' – is typical, but vesting schedules can vary from startup to startup.

The feeling of ownership founders have around their ideas can create negative emotions around vesting. 'I poured myself into starting this company – what do you mean I get nothing?' But the minute they start to think of themselves not as the person that leaves but as the person who *stays*, it starts to feel like a very good idea. Vesting is one of the most important founder protections you can have when legally establishing a company. It helps to resolve the question about equity split. You might start 50/50, but if someone isn't pulling their weight, and they leave, their ownership will fall. That way, the value is weighted by who actually does the work over a period of time, rather than trying to decide how much the work you've done in the past should translate to the value you get in the future.

What Our Founders Say

Break Up Fast

Founder Maria Meier, CTO and co-founder of Phantasma Labs in Berlin, broke up with other founders multiple times before she found the right fit. She followed her gut when it came to deciding on a partner: 'That was really important to me – if it didn't feel right, to break up immediately.' While it was stressful for her because she naturally wondered if she would ever find a partner, she eventually connected with Ramakrishna Nanjundaiah, and their level of productivity helped her realize it was the right fit. Phantasma, a company modelling human motion for safety-critical applications such as autonomous driving and other modes of future mobility, was born. 'I'm surprised every day by how much we can achieve together in such a short amount of time,' she said.

Wait for That Landmine Feeling

'It took me six teams to find my co-founder Raphael [Holca-Lamarre],' said founder Tuhin Chakraborty, CEO of Mimica in London, which builds self-learning automations for digital work. 'We'd met multiple times and spent many hours brainstorming. We worked exceptionally well together but didn't have the right idea. When he came to me with a vision for our company, Mimica, it took off.' It was the constant iteration of an idea *and* of a relationship that eventually led to a payoff. 'Iterate on one or both until it clicks. I read somewhere that finding product/market fit feels like stepping on a landmine. The moment you find the right co-founder is similar.'

It's Not All About You

When founders search for their ideal partner, they naturally focus on finding someone who is a good fit for them. But don't forget, you must also be a good fit for your partner. Ed-tech entrepreneur Jesse Lozano noticed early on that he had to look at himself objectively and ensure that he was capable of being a great partner to someone else. 'It meant moulding myself into one half of an unstoppable force,' said the pi-top CEO, now based in Texas, USA. He looked at positive characteristics from other founders around him and did his best to emulate them until they became a part of him. 'Always remember that it's not about what your co-founder can do for you – it's about what you can do for your co-founder. How great can you be? How much value can you bring to the table?'

Chapter Summary

The only way to test a co-founder is to start working together. Early-stage productivity is measured by how quickly your team can learn. Functional teams are eager to share discoveries and update their hypotheses together.

- Productivity is traction for teams. Focus on the speed at which you can learn alongside your co-founder.
- If you don't find a strong cadence in your early work together, break up quickly.
- Front-load the partnership with fierce conversations. Voicing your expectations and keeping each other accountable is essential for building trust.
- Figure out your equity split and agreed vesting schedule early on to build your foundations and protect yourselves from fall-outs.

CHAPTER 10

Getting to Founder/Idea Fit

*You never change things by fighting the existing reality.
To change something, build a new model that makes the
existing model obsolete.*
Buckminster Fuller

A great startup creates new facts about the world. If you already know who the customer is, exactly what they want, what they'll pay and how to reach them, you're likely describing a company that already exists. If everything about the problem is known, the opportunity is gone.

That said, startups shouldn't try to be totally new in every dimension. The challenge with big ideas is defining them well enough to make sure they actually map to the real world. One way to think about a startup is that you're taking a belief about what the world *could* be and gradually building that possibility into existence.

Big ideas are built from small starts, but if you read the startup press, it's almost as if ideas are floating around, and you can simply pluck one out of thin air, fully formed. Too many people delay founding because they buy into these myths. They don't see themselves as a genius with the 'perfect idea'.

This mythology is misleading. There is no such thing as an objectively good idea or an independently exceptional founder. Having watched the process unfold thousands of times, we have seen that ideation is a process you can learn. It is founder/idea fit that makes a company successful, and we've developed a framework to fast-track that discovery process. Your idea is not a fixed entity; it's a journey. It will and should change drastically because it will be influenced by what you learn from customers in real-time.

A core part of our philosophy is that founders should be developing an idea *with* a co-founder rather than finding a co-founder *for* an idea. This is reflected in our ideation framework.

Our approach to bringing an idea to life is based on our extensive experience turning cohorts of exceptional individuals into highly effective teams. We've found that, unless you provide some constraints for ideation, it's very hard for people to come up with an idea when prompted. What's more, having a structure to guide your thoughts and actions will enable you to simultaneously test an idea and the co-founder relationship. It's not the only way to found, and we cannot guarantee that by using this framework you will succeed, but we hope that our four-phase process will help you minimize your likelihood of making common mistakes and give you the best chance of success. As Sachin Chiramel, founder of Real Analytics in Bangalore, said, 'There will never be a perfect time, and there will rarely be a perfect idea. Instead of waiting for the perfect time and for a fully baked idea, start ideating immediately with your co-founder, and validating or invalidating ideas fast.'

EF Ideation Framework

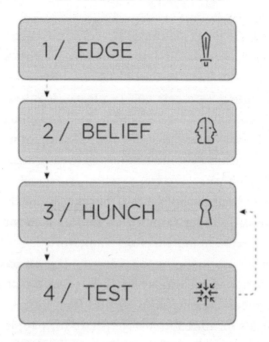

Phase One: Leverage your Edge [Timeline: a couple of days]
Identifying your primary Edge gives you the strongest starting point for ideation. By using your Edge, you focus on using your existing knowledge and skills to your advantage. It should give you a head start as you already have a baseline of knowledge about the area you're going after. More importantly, it also provides a constraint, and constraints are proven to increase creativity when developing ideas. Researchers looked at 145 empirical studies on how constraints affect innovation and found that 'when there are no constraints on the creative process, complacency sets in'. Without constraints, people tend to follow the path-of-least-resistance. 'They go for the most intuitive idea that comes to mind rather than investing in the development of better ideas.'[13] Patricia Stokes

---

[13] Acar, Oguz A., Murat Tarakci, and Daan van Knippenberg. 'Why Constraints Are Good for Innovation'. *Harvard Business Review*, November 22, 2019. https://hbr.org/2019/11/why -constraints-are-good-for-innovation

argues in her book *Creativity from Constraints: The Psychology of Breakthrough* that moving from mastery to creativity comes when new constraints are imposed on an area you know well.[14] Science backs this up. Researchers found that with an abundance of options, people have less incentive to use their resources in new and creative ways. However, when faced with scarcity – constraints – test subjects gave themselves the freedom to use their resources in unconventional ways.[15] Constraints are too often perceived negatively when they are a quick way to increase creativity. Constraints can broaden your perception and create new pathways for novel thinking.

If you think of co-founding with Edge as playing a partnered card game, you want to combine your most valuable, highly developed Edge with someone else's. This provides an interesting and often unique set of constraints to ideate within. This combinatorial innovation should, counterintuitively, increase the volume and quality of possible ideas.

Steve Jobs once said that 'creativity is just connecting things'. Combinatorial innovation is the essence of creativity, meaning that even though we believe we've come up with a novel idea, those 'eureka moments' are actually a function of neural connections being made between pre-existing ideas and knowledge. Our brains are constantly consolidating information, and the spark of innovation we feel is inspired by innumerable insights accumulated over years.

If both you and your co-founder have a relative Edge on a distinct dimension, then chances are your joint Edge is significant. Take Zeena and John: Zeena was five years out of university where,

[14] Oppong, Thomas. 'For A More Creative Brain, Embrace Constraints'. Inc.com, November 30, 2017. https://www.inc.com/thomas-oppong/for-a-more-creative-brain-embrace -constraints.html.
[15] Mehta, Ravi, and Zhu, Meng. 'Creating When You Have Less: The Impact of Resource Scarcity on Product Use Creativity'. *Journal of Consumer Research* 42, no. 5 (February 1, 2016): 767–82. https://doi.org/10.1093/jcr/ucv051.

alongside her degree, she had also trained in Applied Behaviour Analysis Therapy. John had a master's degree in sound computing and thought of himself as an audiophile. Zeena and John started talking about their Edges, and it turned out that John's previous work touched on voice performance in films, but he wasn't sure of where to apply the speech technology he created until he learned that Zeena had spent most of her young adult life in a part-time role supporting kids with speech difficulties who played video games. She had learned an incredible amount about how speech is developed through that experience. Exploring the intersection of their Edges led to the idea to build Sonantic, a startup that uses AI to create hyper-realistic synthetic voices for gaming and entertainment studios.

Phase 2: Articulate your beliefs [Timeline: 2–48 hours]

One of the challenges of having an 'idea' is that the word encompasses two things. One, it's what you hope to achieve in the long term – the mission and vision for the company to which you'll dedicate a significant portion of your life. Two, it needs to communicate the here and now. What will you do now to show that you are able to create real value in the short term? To acknowledge this distinction, we don't talk about ideas. Instead, we differentiate between having a 'belief' (the long-term vision) and a 'hunch' (how you bring that to life today).

A joint, core belief is the building block of a co-founding team. Beliefs are the North Star for the founders that ensure you remember the *why* behind what you are doing. Startups change, pivot and iterate. However, founding beliefs should remain consistent. They are a high-level description of the change you want to make in the world. For EF, our founding belief is that the world is missing out on some of its best founders. There are many ways for us to bring that belief to life – and we have tried many of them! – but fundamentally, the 'why' behind the company has remained consistent for over ten years. The 'how' has evolved and expanded over time and now includes this book. These pages are a tool to reach a global audience at a scale far beyond our programme cohorts, in places we would not otherwise be able to access.

In the initial stages of building a co-founding team, the belief phase is an opportunity to deeply understand the interest areas of your potential partner in a short amount of time. Within a couple of hours of discussing beliefs with someone, you should have a view of whether your interests overlap and if you share similar views about what the future might look like.

The questions you should ask together include:

- Based on your combined Edges, what do you believe could be different about a market, an industry or the world in five years' time?
- How do you believe people or companies will behave differently in the future because of your belief?
- Will that vision fuel you both for the next five to ten years?

You might start big and wide, for example, by applying a technology across many different fields, or you might start from a particular insight about how a market will look different in the future. The strongest beliefs are often linked to a change. This could be a new type of customer behaviour or social change, a regulatory change or a technological change. Niklas Zennström, co-founder of Skype and now Founding Partner and CEO of VC Atomico, said of belief, 'My co-founder and I had some ideas that were similar and complementary. We both shared the belief that the internet would be huge. This was in 1997!' Their radical belief about the internet's possibilities in telephony underpinned the idea for Skype which, three years after founding, had 100 million users. 'We realized we could displace the global telephony network with a peer-to-peer app using an evolution of the technology we had used at our previous startups, and that could be a game changer. The big unknown was whether people would sit in front of their computers making phone calls,' reflected Zennström. Great founders can develop a belief that creates a story about how the change they're seeing now can lead to a huge future opportunity, including the potential creation of brand new markets.

These conversations should be energizing. In fact, they can be so energizing that potential co-founding pairs get bogged down in this stage. Coming up with new beliefs for days on end isn't an indicator of success. The best teams are able to align on a common belief within the first day of working together. They then explore that belief together, digging into the details and looking for signs of misalignment between the co-founders. It can be easy to agree on the surface about a belief, particularly one that is contentious or extreme. To find a true partner, push into the details to ensure you're aligned. 'In the beginning, every idea seems revolutionary, but it's with the details that it gets complicated, and you realize there is a rocky path ahead,' said Leo Spenner, co-founder of Alcemy, Berlin.

Be honest about early indicators that you're not suited to work together. If the beliefs that arise between you do not excite you, it's a signal you're not on the right team. If you like someone's personality but you're compromising on the strength of an idea, it's not the right trade-off to make. Not all shared beliefs yield successful teams. If you go out and disprove your core belief with customers or you lose excitement about it as a team, and you can't align on a new belief fast, it's time to break up.

Phase 3: Agree on a hunch [Timeline: 1–3 days]

If you're aligned in your beliefs (the vision), the co-founder conversation then shifts to developing a hunch (how you'll get there). A hunch is a hypothesis about what core problem you're going to solve and what solution you could build to solve it. If you were to have a hunch about how your team's belief could be brought to reality, what would that be? We use the word hunch because, before you have tested it with customers, it is a guess at best. As much as you might know the market or problem, your fledgling idea is still stacked with uncertainty until you have deeply explored it with customers.

Some questions to pose at this phase:

- How would you frame your belief as a problem experienced by potential users or customers? Who are those potential users or customers that care about this problem the most?
- What's your hunch about how potential users or customers experience this problem today?
- What's your hunch about how you could potentially solve this problem for them now?

When building a startup, learning is your number-one goal – you're starting with countless unknowns. In the beginning, you will be testing aspects of the hunch to determine if they are true. Note that neither the problem nor the solution is fixed. Your initial hunch comes from your intuitive answers to those questions. You will constantly update your hunch based on new information. The strongest teams will balance short-term learning while maintaining long-term vision. Your hunch will evolve and become more precise over time. 'There's a real force when you find someone who has complete belief in the company they are building without the conviction of their own ideas [hunches] – because ideally, they're fairly egoless and willing to adapt and change,' said Rob Bishop, co-founder and CEO of Magic Pony Technology and Product Management VP at Twitter.

We use the phrase 'strong hunches, weakly held' to describe how you should think about your hunch. You should have a firm belief in your initial hunch and feel confident that you have reasonably and precisely explained the problem and solution you have in mind. And when you start getting new information that contradicts, challenges or confirms your hunch, you quickly update it.

Some founders who don't have strong conviction in their hunch try to 'crowdsource' one instead. Speaking to customers can be misinterpreted as 'get the customer to tell you what they want'. We see early-stage founders diligently lining up hundreds of customer interviews and then trying to synthesize this mass of 'data' into a product. This is impossible. Lean methodology is not about asking customers what they want but about bringing clear and well-structured hunches to the table that you can test with customers (we'll explore customer development in much greater detail in our next chapter).

Phase 4: Test with customers [Timeline: continuous, but with weekly review points]

Once you have created a hunch about the problem and the potential solution that you could create, it's time to test. Remember that during this phase, you are testing two things: your nascent idea and your co-founder.

In *The Lean Startup*, author Eric Ries popularized the idea of using customer feedback to understand the demand for the product and then using that to iterate and refine your value proposition. During this stage, the priority should be customer understanding – not pitching a perfect product or proving that you're right about your hunch. The 'winning' idea will often come from what you learn about your customers along the way – insights you uncover whilst testing the 'losing' hunch. And remember, the learning process is meant to enhance your Edge. Throughout this process, you are essentially building a moat of knowledge with which to defend your business.

Some questions to pose at this phase:

- What's the smallest thing you can do to test whether your idea has potential? Whom should you speak to?
- What's the minimum viable information (short, important and focused) you need to understand the viability of your hunch? What do you need to know to ensure that your idea has potential?

- What's the assumption that carries the highest risk to your company? What would we need to hear from a customer to kill this idea?
- What do you need to learn from customer interactions that will allow you to edit and update your 'hunch'?

All of these questions are best answered by speaking to customers, which we'll cover in the next chapter.

Building the habit of speaking to customers and learning from Day One sets you up for success in the long term. As the entrepreneur and author Steve Blank (*Four Steps to the Epiphany* and *The Startup Owner's Manual*) said, startups don't just do what big companies do on a smaller scale. Instead of executing on a business model, startups function as a temporary organization that exists to search for a *new* business model. Learning is important because, for a successful startup, you have to find a model that hasn't previously existed in its full form. This requires experimentation, testing and a constant openness to learning.

Understanding the Idea Maze

As founders start the process of testing their hunches, we encourage them to go through the Idea Maze. This is a concept set out by Balaji Srinivasan, a serial entrepreneur who said:

> A good founder is capable of anticipating which turns lead to treasure and which lead to certain death. A bad founder is just running to the entrance of (say) the 'movies/music/file-sharing/P2P' maze or the 'photo-sharing' maze without any sense for the history of the industry, the players in the maze, the casualties of the past, and the technologies that are likely to move walls and change assumptions.

Visualize your idea at the end of the maze. Acknowledge that there will be false starts, wrong turns and a long, uncertain road to the finish line. As a founder, it is very tempting to only look forward, but there is much to learn from understanding the history of an industry or an idea. If someone had already completed part of the maze, wouldn't you want to learn from them? The hunch you're developing has probably been tried and tested by someone else to varying degrees of success. Short-cut your path forward by taking the time to learn from what's happened in the past.

Chris Dixon, an investor at Andreessen Horowitz, details two ways founders should explore the Idea Maze:

1. **History.** The internet gives you access to what current and former attempts at this idea have looked like. You should understand what they did right and what they did wrong. If you're building a social network, you should understand the history of the space, such as why Facebook was able to displace MySpace so quickly or why TikTok's route to market was through existing platforms such as Instagram. You can also learn why someone hasn't already built the idea.
2. **Analogy.** Don't constrain your understanding of the Idea Maze. Analogous businesses, ideas and industries can have useful nuggets of learning. If you're building a marketplace, you should understand what you can learn from eBay, even if you're going after a different customer group.

As an investor, founders who truly understand and are curious about their Idea Maze come across as far more sophisticated than those who don't. At a basic level, it's frustrating in an investment meeting if you ask a founder about another well-known company in the space they're working in, and they look at you blankly. You want to project a degree of expertise in a pitch meeting; having done your homework gives you credibility, even if you're a newcomer to an industry.

Chris Dixon recommends speaking to experienced founders or investors about your idea. Although you can find write-ups of how different ideas have performed, the real gems of information will often be in people's heads, not published articles. 'The benefits of learning about the maze generally far outweigh the risks of having your idea stolen,' he said.

Examples of the EF Ideation Framework in Practice

Matt Wilson and Guenther Eisinger are now the co-founders of Omnipresent. They started building Omnipresent at the beginning of the pandemic. The world was changing fast around them, and they had a belief that the shift to working from home would not just be permanent but would create a new generation of remote-first companies. They had a hunch that legally, financially and technically employing people around the world would be a significant barrier to this change happening, and they thought they could fix it. Their testing with customers showed that employee onboarding, particularly with employees living all over the world, was a hair on fire problem and that existing solutions were expensive and inadequate. Matt and Guenther went from being strangers to co-founders of a company that had raised its Series A just twelve months later.

When Rayna Patel and Georgina Kirby founded VineHealth in London, they were ideating off Edges in clinical medicine, behavioural and cognitive science, data science, AI technologies and remote-sensing data collection. Their shared belief was that drug development is outdated, slow, expensive and creates drugs that 1) don't prioritize the outcomes that matter to patients and 2) don't have the real-world effects that we are led to expect from trials. They built an AI-driven app to replace often inaccurate clinician-generated data regarding symptoms and quality of life.

'We believed that if you could encapsulate this data collection into a system that delivered value to patients – that helped them manage their condition day-to-day and actively supported them – you could collect much richer and more meaningful data,' Rayna said.

Their product is a win for patients, who receive more personalized care. It's also a win for hospitals and pharmaceutical companies that can use the data to differentiate between otherwise similar classes of medications, inform regulation, use AI to identify clinically relevant patterns and deliver precise and automated patient engagement.

Testing your Co-founder and the Idea

As you focus on testing your hunch, keep in mind that you're also testing the foundation of your startup – the co-founding team. Each opportunity to reflect together on the information you get from customer development offers insights into your co-founder relationship. Do you talk over each other when discussing and debating how to update your hunch, or do you defer and retreat? How do you deal with impasses and tough decision-making? How do you leverage each other's areas of expertise?

What you're looking for is a co-founder who pushes you to be the best version of yourself. You are not looking for someone with whom you agree on every decision. You should have the ability to debate and discuss your ideas so you arrive at a better conclusion. Ideally, you will remind each other that neither of you has the answer. The only person who has the answer is the customer. In disagreements, the customer should break the deadlock.

Your team should move from test to updated hunch to test to updated hunch. You will move through this process until you reach Product-Market Fit. As Toby Mather, co-founder of Lingumi, says, 'Fixate on the vision. Flex on the journey.'

A Note on Timelines

One element that surprises people about our framework is the speed at which we expect new founders to move through the team formation and ideation process. It's easy to believe that with more time, you can gather more information to make a good assessment of your idea or your co-founder. In reality, you can never have enough information to have full confidence in your decision. Instead, look for sufficient information and evidence to help you make a judgement call. Know what behaviours are red flags for you, and have confidence in your deal breakers.

By focusing on finding sufficient information – rather than perfect information – you will reduce the time it takes to evaluate your team and idea. Ideally, you want to break up with a co-founder or change a hunch/belief before you have created significant assets. The more assets you create, the harder it is to stop – even if you know that you're not in the right co-founding team or working on the right idea. The sunk cost fallacy is real.

As Peter Thiel, co-founder of PayPal, Palantir and the first outside investor in Facebook, said, the sweet spot for startups is the intersection between good ideas and things that sound like bad ideas. If someone had come to us with Airbnb, we could have pointed out many reasons why it wouldn't work – that's the easy part. The hard part is seeing opportunity and not just believing in it but gathering evidence to take others on the journey. Remember that apart from your customers, no one can tell you that your idea is bad.

Chapter Summary

Founder/idea fit makes a company successful; developing an idea *with* a co-founder rather than finding a co-founder *for* an idea is key to fast-tracking that process.

- Starting from Edge turns constraints into creativity through combinatorial innovation.
- Define a belief that speaks to the essence of why you are founding a company together.

- Develop a hunch that establishes a hypothesis and 'what if' around a problem, which you will continuously refine through testing.
- Understand where other companies within your field have succeeded and failed, so you can work from an existing knowledge of the landscape.

CHAPTER 11

Customer Development – Finding Out Your Customer's Secrets

To build a startup that makes it out of infancy, you must understand your customer. There are no shortcuts. Your opportunity exists as a founder because of uncertainty. Customer development is about homing in on the insight that allows you to gradually reduce uncertainty. It's the first step toward product-market fit – when your product satisfies your customer and their needs.

Speaking to the customer is how you find out the insights or 'secrets' that underpin the world's best startups. They're often referred to as secrets because the best founders find out something about their customer that others hadn't – and sometimes secrets that the customer didn't even know about themselves.

If your insight is obvious, you are probably entering a very competitive market. Think about the food delivery market, companies like Deliveroo, Wolt and foodpanda. It was obvious that many city dwellers would like more convenient ways to have their food delivered. A couple of very big companies were built in this space, but the market became hyper-competitive and margins too thin. The more you can find an insight that is hidden away in how a customer thinks about a problem, the more likely you are to build something that not only meets their needs but outperforms every alternative.

You discover your customers' secrets through significant time spent speaking to and observing your customer. It should be done in two phases: customer discovery and customer development.

Customer discovery is the search and test phase. Customer development is the refinement phase. Customer discovery happens in the very early stages of your startup when your hunch is barely formed. In customer discovery, you speak to customers to understand their motivations and behaviours. Your first job as a founder is to go out and speak to as many potential users as it takes to understand their secret. The targeted questions you ask will help you develop an understanding of their problems, their nuanced motivations and what substitutes or other solutions they have used to fix that problem. You then use this information to update your hunch. If you already have deep knowledge of the problem through your Edge, customer discovery might happen quickly. If not, discovery could take days, weeks or months before you have confidence in your hunch.

Customer development answers the question: 'Is this a good idea?' You're taking your hunch to the customer to be validated. As you will soon find out, many of your family and friends will freely give you their opinion (whether you request it or not) and tell you whether you have a 'good' idea or a 'bad' idea, but the only people you should listen to are potential customers or users of your product. Putting your early prototype out to customers, getting feedback and watching how they use it will be a core part of your role as a founder in the early days. The best startups continue this customer-focused behaviour to product-market fit and beyond.

Founders can sometimes feel 'held up' by the need to speak to customers. They're keen to get building and get selling. Customer development came about in response to the enormous startup failures of the early 2000s, where billions of venture capital funds were invested in fully formed companies that were building products customers didn't want. Customer development gives you the best chance to avoid building something no one wants.

Rob Fitzpatrick, author of *The Mom Test*, argues that 'Customer development is incredibly time-efficient compared to something like building a prototype. It doesn't answer every question, but the questions that it does answer it answers very quickly.' For every hour of customer development time, you could save tens of hours of programming time in the future. However, sometimes customer development can often seem like a waste of time because founders ask the wrong questions or ask in the wrong way. 'The "data" can get very muddied. Customer development is a tool you need to learn how to use otherwise it can backfire,' Fitzpatrick said.

Customer Discovery in Practice

Once you have developed your hunch with your co-founder you need to start customer discovery. It's time to 'get out of the building', as Steve Blank, serial entrepreneur and father of the Lean Startup Movement, says. This means that it's time to step away from your desks and start speaking to the customer.

The key word in that sentence is 'speak'. It can be tempting to start using surveys to try and build a quantitative dataset of your customers' needs and motivations. Surveys are an inadequate tool for customer discovery. 'Surveys can't tell you the emotional makeup of your customers, it can't tell you their decision-making process, it can't tell you why they're doing it this way instead of that. You want to run conversational interviews, it should be like talking to a friend,' said Fitzpatrick.

'Every single one of you reading this already knows how to run a perfect customer interview if you have at least one friend. Because the way that we build friendships, and the way we build relationships is by getting to understand another person. If you sat down with your friend, and they said, "Man, I just got dumped" you wouldn't say, "Excellent. I want to understand on a scale of 1 to 10 how upset does this make you? How likely are you to download a dating app in the next 30 days?"'

Fitzpatrick encourages founders to respond as they would to a friend. 'Wow, that sucks. Tell me everything. What happened? Talk me through it. What are you going to do next?' These simple yet powerful questions can feel overly emotional for a business conversation, but the best products tap into an emotional need as well as a functional requirement.

This is something that investors look for, too. Sara Clemens, COO of Twitch and angel investor, said that 'all of the ideas that seem game-changing come back to a human need. We want to be connected, entertained, educated. The best ideas tap into elements of Maslow's hierarchy of needs.' Maslow's hierarchy prioritizes human needs, starting with physiological needs followed by safety, love, esteem and then self-actualization. Founders should think of customer development as an opportunity to really dig into a customer's psyche. This is where the secrets are.

You might have a hunch that solves a known problem that customers can articulate. For example, search engines in the early 2000s sucked. They were covered in adverts and gave lacklustre search results. Google's search algorithm solved this known problem. The market for search engines already existed, and customer development would have highlighted users' issues with the existing product and workflow. If you're building a product for a known problem, by deeply understanding the customer's experience and mindset, you increase your chance of producing a superior solution.

Alternatively, you might be trying to tap into a new behaviour that doesn't exist or isn't embedded yet. Take a product like Snapchat which created a whole new user behaviour around ephemeral messaging. This is unlikely a problem that the customer could have articulated. However, proper customer discovery could have unearthed teenagers' frustrations at the permanence of the messages they sent to each other.

Another simple way to deeply understand your customer is to watch them in action. Humans are very poor at understanding themselves, whether it be knowing how they use their time or knowing what their preferences are. By spending time observing them, you can get higher-quality insights into their true motivations. Frederick Sia and Admond Lee, co-founders of Gigstaq, were building a product for delivery riders in Singapore. To observe their customers in action and discover their secrets, they became delivery riders themselves.

This qualitative approach can be frustrating for data-driven individuals because all you'll ever have is indications. You'll never have the firm conclusions and statistics you're used to. Facts + experience = data. You're taking in anecdotal information and using the filter of your Edges to understand what it means for your hunch.

When trying to work out who to contact, look for people who have a 'hair on fire' problem. Imagine, if your hair was on fire – you'd be desperate to get it solved and would probably be willing to respond to a cold message from a stranger. Part of developing your hunch is not only outlining the problem but having a hunch about who might be the early adopter.

In the early days, customer outreach will be laughably manual. Don't take a low response rate as an indication of low demand. You are trying to find the individuals who will say yes. Out of 5,000 cold emails, you might achieve (idealistically) a 10 per cent reply rate. Say 25 per cent of those respondents indicate they are interested in your idea. You might initiate 125 email conversations, 20 per cent of whom want a follow-up meeting. Remember, never assume someone won't give you the time of day because of their stature. Likewise, don't assume an industry leader is the closest to your problem.

Out of those twenty-five meetings, perhaps 20 per cent are the 'hair on fire' customers you're looking for. That's only five people. But those five can be priceless. When you find them, ask them for warm introductions to others in the same spheres. Ask them, 'Who else can we speak to? Do you mind introducing us?' This is a great indicator that they're truly interested because if they nod their heads throughout the meeting but aren't willing to introduce you to one of their connections, how much do they really care about the problem you're solving? As with finding a co-founder, you're looking for those bridge contacts who can connect you to other warm networks of similar individuals.

Zeena Qureshi, co-founder of Sonantic in London, spoke to 500 games developers in the first three months of founding (and she reached out to many more on LinkedIn who never responded). She and her co-founder, John, had a hunch that his emotional speech technology could be used in the gaming market. Neither had deep experience of this market, but Zeena had sufficient experience to know that there was a problem that needed to be solved, and John came from the world of Hollywood, a very close adjacency. In conversation with games developers, she was able to home in on the exact problem of keeping within budget and timelines when developing voice for games. With every conversation, their understanding of the problem became deeper and clearer. They started hearing the same problem framed again and again, giving John and Zeena the confidence to start product development. All their eventual pilots came from the cold outreach they had done on LinkedIn.

Or take Alexandra Boussommier-Calleja, founder of ImVitro in Paris, who said:

> We did a lot of cold approaches via LinkedIn, or cold emails by finding the contact details of scientists on their publications. I believe that the fact that I was an outsider to the IVF world helped a lot: I wasn't selling myself as an IVF expert, but as someone who has gathered expertise somewhere else, which could be applied to their current challenges. I reached out to about 120 fertility centres and doctors and probably talked to 40 of them. When I obtained around ten letters of intent (LOIs), I felt confident that the need was real, especially after having visited many clinics and doctors and seeing how much time busy doctors were willing to put into this project.

Keep in mind that this is not sales. When reaching out to potential customers, you are not trying to sign them up in your initial email or message. An easy way to position yourself in your cold outreach is that you're looking for help to understand something. Position the person you're reaching out to, whether it's a startup employee, a child or a CXO, as an expert that you want to learn from. You'll be amazed at the response very senior people will give to interesting startups who want to chat. Give them something that it's really easy for them to say 'yes' to. It's not hard to agree to give you five minutes to speak on the phone. On the call, pique their interest enough that they will agree to a longer discussion. 'People love talking about themselves and their frustrations. You don't need to be that good at this. As long as you keep bringing it back to them, you're going to get the learning you need,' Fitzpatrick said.

We'll say it one more time. This is not sales. It's important that you don't share your hunch with the customer during discovery. By sharing your hunch too early, you're likely to fall foul to customers' kind human nature where they give you platitudes about how great it's going to be. Even when you feel ready to move on to customer development and show early mock-ups or prototypes of your product, you still aren't selling. You're trying to get genuine feedback from the customer on whether and how they would use it.

If you get turned down, don't take it personally. 'You have to separate yourself from your company to help you manage the no's,' advises Paris-based Kinetix co-founder Yassine Tahi. There is no such thing as rejection in customer development because tough moments provide you with an opportunity to learn. The same factors that make this kind of outreach frustrating fuel your right to win. Not many people will go to the same lengths to get to know their customers.

Customer Development in Practice

You don't need a product in order to speak to customers. In fact, it can be worse if you show them one. Customers become blinded by your product and its current capabilities, which skews their response. When you lead with questions designed to support an existing product, it's easier for customers to lie because they either don't want to hurt your feelings, or they are all too willing to be happily led to your solution. Avoid these questions:

- Do you think it's a good idea?
- Would you ever buy a solution like this?
- Wouldn't all these features be really useful?
- How much would you pay for this?

In customer conversations, you don't want direct feedback on your idea. Instead, look for actionable insights about someone's industry, company and day-to-day work. Ground your probing in specific examples:

- Why do you do this?
- Talk me through the last time that happened?
- Why does this matter?
- What else have you tried?

If they've searched for alternative solutions that *nearly* work but leave them frustrated, this is an indication of genuine need. Follow the emotion, and let it rub off on you and fuel your drive to create a solution. Empathetic founders express disbelief that somebody's processes could be plagued with this level of inefficiency. Hair-on-fire problems leave you wondering, 'How can it be that in this decade, people are still dealing with…?'

Once you are hearing the same responses again and again and beginning to see a pattern in how the customer is talking about the problem, it's time to move to customer development. Elizabeth Chan, co-founder of Sequoia-backed Neptune Robotics, said that 'After talking to hundreds of people, we finally saw a clear pattern in their pain. Once we started solving a small percentage of their pain with our MVP [Minimum Viable Product], our potential customers started to trust us and get excited.'

Your goal now is to refine your hunch. If you think about customer discovery as casting a wide net, customer development is about going deep with people who you think could be your customers.

In customer development, you can start sharing an MVP with your customers. An MVP is the smallest (and often scrappiest!) version of your product that allows you to understand how the customer will interact with it. An MVP can be as small as a mock-up, a light-featured app or a human-in-the-loop experience.

Satisfying the requirements for quality and quantity feedback depends on the kind of business you're building. If you're developing a B2B (business to business) or enterprise-facing product, going really deep with a handful of customers to understand their problem could be sufficient without an MVP. If you're doing something that is consumer-facing, you will likely need a couple hundred customers using an early prototype.

If you're building something that is tech-enabled and very easy to bring to market, there's no reason why you can't get them to use the very first versions of your product during customer development. Watch them in action. Try and get them to work through what your hunch is of the product and get that immediate feedback. When companies are raising seed for a B2C (business to consumer) product, investors' eyes will light up when the founders share a hacky prototype that has a couple of hundred people using it on a daily basis.

If you have a very complex product using advanced technology that might take six to twelve months to build, the challenge is to do customer development without ever actually getting them to use the product. Consider alternative ways for them to experiment with the product – through mock-ups or by embedding yourself in the organization to be the human version of the product – and understand every facet of what it would take for them to not just be interested in your product but to become a user and a customer.

One of the issues with putting out an MVP too early is that founders can become too attached to their creations. In particular, if you've delivered a true mock-up style MVP rather than something hacked together, you must be incredibly disciplined to use customer development to iterate into the next version. That may mean completely dismantling and destroying everything you've built.

For this reason, we see founders resist getting the MVP out there when they need to as they move from discovery to development. For those who have a more fixed mindset (a concept coined by Carol Dweck) in particular, there's a mental barrier to having that first interaction with a customer. There's hesitation around presenting something that could be dismissed.

On the flip side, overconfidence in the MVP turns it into something to sell rather than something to truly learn from. One of the hardest things about doing customer development, especially after you have a product, is the temptation to sell. Get out of your sales mindset and poke and prod at their sore spot. You're trying to diagnose the problem and get the customer to articulate the source and impact of their pain so that you can translate your understanding into a prototype.

Running into the Spike

Loving your customer is the avenue to understanding the deepest problems of your idea. Customer development isn't about getting to 'yes'. That's a sales strategy. It's also not about getting to 'no'. No is the starting point. There is no such thing as rejection in customer development because tough moments provide you with an opportunity to learn.

When we say 'running into the spike', we mean that you run directly at the scariest and thorniest problem with your idea. It means you ask the question that might kill your startup. The truth is that most startup ideas are bad. You can either find out early on, or you can put it off (out of fear or avoidance) and come to that conclusion after you've dumped time, money and energy into it. Founders avoid the spike when they stay in their comfort zone and speak to friends and colleagues about the idea rather than reaching out to the customer. Even if those close connections are possible users of the product, they will probably give you filtered and positive feedback. They don't hold the spike.

The spike runs all the way through to the marketplace. It's likely that one of the sides of your marketplace – either your supply-side or your demand-side – will be much, much harder to bring to the table than the other. It's easy to get distracted by the easy side of the market because that's where the traction is. But that's a mistake. Returning to the example of Airbnb, it wasn't hard to find people who were interested in making money on rooms they already paid for. The real challenge was on the demand side: could they get people to stay in a stranger's house? They had to run straight into that spike head on.

Unless you're running into the spike from the get-go by asking the right questions to your hair-on-fire customers, you won't generate the insights you need to build the best product to solve the problem. Don't hang on to the idea and protect it. You are not your idea. You are not your company. You can start many companies. There are many ideas you can have. So if this is the wrong idea, don't make it part of your identity. Run into the spike. Kill it off, and move on to the next one.

A Case Study

Dishpatch, which enables the UK's best restaurants to produce, sell and deliver finish-at-home meal kits, was conceived in the early days of pandemic lockdown. Co-founders Pete Butler, CEO, and James Terry,

CPO, used their combined Edges in restaurant knowledge and product development to quickly launch what began as a wholesale grocery directory. They generated over £30,000 of sales in the first eight weeks of operation. Butler describes their MVP as averagely successful. 'We sold some products, and some people quite liked us, but we knew that we hadn't really nailed the problem on the consumer side or the problem on the supply side,' he said.

Customer interviews helped them map a step-by-step journey and pin down pain points that illuminated new opportunities. They soon moved from a simple but useful directory into a drop-ship model to capture the value of facilitating transactions through their site.

'Based on the aggregation of problem areas, we then rebuilt our own hypothesis and the potential solutions we can build,' Butler said. 'The solution shouldn't be something that solves all problems. It's not a gymnastics score; you don't get any prizes for complexity. You do something simple that allows you to do something else and then something else, and that opens up a big opportunity.'

'You can zoom right in and figure out how you better solve a specific problem that you're going after,' Butler added. 'Or, you can zoom out a little bit, and say, "OK, maybe we're not solving the right problem here."'

They refined their hunch to centre in the space adjacent to groceries: restaurant deliveries and meal kits. 'It took us a bit of time to build confidence to move to that, but the more we thought about it, the more obvious it became,' Butler said. 'We had this hunch, based on working in restaurants for so long, that restaurants are never going to make these things themselves. And we can basically do it all for them.'

The team recognized that they needed to make a big pivot but saw the risk of losing what they had already built. So, they tested the meal kit directory idea as a subsite. When they sold more meal kits in a week than they had in their drop-ship model over the previous three months, they knew they had found the right match between problem and solution.

'The biggest mistake I see people make is that they launch MVPs that don't work,' Butler said. 'Your MVP is a wedge, and therefore, it has to have standalone value from the first day. The best way to do that is to really focus on one problem and solve that simply. That is your wedge into all the adjacent problems, and everything else in that problem space.'

Dishpatch went on to raise their seed round from one of the world's best VCs, Andreessen Horowitz, just a few months after launching their product.

Life is Too Short to Build Something Nobody Wants

Generally, the market is the make-or-break factor for even the strongest co-founding teams. When you think about many of the high-profile failures from the early 2000s, a big factor in their downfall was that they built something people didn't want. They built whole infrastructures and businesses around very good ideas that were before their time. The first online grocery store raised billions and billions of dollars. Yet they tanked pretty quickly after they launched because not enough people were able or willing to put their payment details online. A decade and a half later, Instacart launched a very similar and highly successful product. If you are going after a small or non-existent market, there is no way you can beat that force. Conversely, in a huge market with pent-up demand, the market can drag the product or solution out of the startup. Founders should be prepared to answer 'Why now?' to prove their idea's time has come.

When a high-powered team meets a strong market, the real magic can happen. The right team can tap into a growing or underserved demand. Entering a huge market, in terms of volume or value, presents a market share challenge. You compete to carve out your slice of the pie.

In a growing market, the pain of a problem might only be felt by a small number today, but if you can see a disruption on the horizon that will exponentially increase demand (say, a global pandemic that completely alters the way people work and live), you can harness that wave.

Tapping into an underserved market with a robust solution for people who've been patching together their own deficient solutions is also an exciting opportunity. Defining your market narrative isn't only about quantitative research and data points. It's about gaining intimate knowledge from customers about the factors driving a problem.

It's important not to confuse customer development – where you uncover insights about your customer problem – with market research. Market research is an attempt to understand the market size. We don't typically think conducting your own market research is especially helpful for startup founders. Market research asks, 'How much money is spent in this way right now?' This approach is more quantitative and top-down, which doesn't lead to insights around opportunities. It's a snapshot of today with some guesses about how the market will grow tomorrow. The goal is to find new and innovative ideas where few people are currently spending money.

You're looking for your early adopters – the people for whom the problem is so sharp and so urgent that their hair is on fire. These people will have the highest tolerance for a product that isn't quite perfect.

The problem is that if you go out and ask people who are not early adopters, they'll tell you there is no market. Imagine doing the survey version of customer development for Airbnb in 2010. Would you stay on a stranger's floor if the hotel rooms were booked up? *No, I wouldn't.* Would I do it now that Airbnb exists? *Yeah, I would.* In other words, Airbnb made the market exist by starting with the early adopters. As a founder, you will have to drag a market into existence.

Your job is to qualitatively say, 'Are the people that are responding to me representative of a big enough group that if these people want it, there is a market?' This does not mean that you reach out to 100 heads of HR, get three replies and determine that only 3 per cent of HR managers will use it. The key is to determine whether those three people replied because they needed a solution yesterday and if a lot of people like them could have this problem.

Now, how do you convince yourself that this is a big market? Interview enough people that you get to the point where you keep hearing the same problems and experiences over and over again. Listen for theme saturation.

The goal is to gather enough knowledge that you can build the minimum viable product (MVP) that gradually brings more of your target market into scope. More people will be willing to engage at that point. But at the start, they are going to be the minority. Your job as a founder is to figure out whether the needs and desires of your early adopters are common enough that the product you're building will draw a larger market.

Linear Ideation

Once you have understood ideation, the Idea Maze and started customer development, you will start invalidating your hunches, updating and upgrading them. It's likely your hunch will change significantly. The Lean Startup movement has made this process of 'pivoting' a standard part of idea development. The pivot has become a positive thing – no longer is it seen as a failure to find yourself working on the wrong idea – it is a founder's badge of honour.

There are two types of pivots – those that destroy value and those that create value. By understanding the difference, founders can fast track their progress towards product-market fit. When you have information from customer development that shows your hunch is wrong, it's time to pivot. Maybe you have failed to find any customers who are excited about your hunch, or maybe you have learnt that the small size of a certain market makes it unattractive.

Some founders react to this by 'pivoting' to a new hunch and belief, i.e., they drop their existing idea in its totality and move on to the next item on their 'idea list'. Often this pivot has no connection to the previous idea that the founders were working on. Not only has the hunch changed, but the fundamental belief behind the business has changed, too. This has a real cost. Every time you pivot in this way, you are discarding important assets that you have created – the knowledge, the contacts and the technology that you have built. You go back to square one every time you pivot like this. It's demotivating and saps founders' energy.

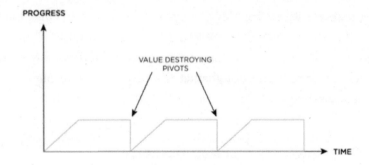

This is a common mistake we see first-time founders make. These aren't pivots – it's basically just starting again.

For example, a founder first tries to tackle improving data analysis for consultants before realizing that consultants already have good in-house systems for this. They then 'pivot' down the idea list and explore making sales teams more effective. It turns out the space is highly competitive. So, they 'pivot' again to a B2C product for advanced athletes. With each pivot, they lose the skills, knowledge and connections they have built and instead start from scratch.

This isn't uncommon and reflects a hunch-focused approach to ideation rather than a 'belief' focus. Every time you return to square one, it becomes less and less likely that you and your co-founder are still fully aligned and excited about the idea. Having a guiding belief at the heart of your ideation process ensures that you and your co-founder remain aligned and excited by what you're doing.

A useful mental model for how to pivot well is to think of it as linear ideation. Linear ideation helps you to recognize and then capitalize on the assets you are creating through the ideation process.

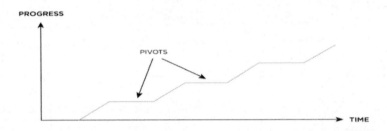

You start with your hunch and go through the usual customer development cycle, seeking input from customers and gathering feedback. You're not looking for your idea to fail; you're looking for the upside – what can you learn from these interactions that allows you to edit and update your idea?

As you spend more and more time in the space, you become a deeper expert. Many founders win by being experts in niche problems. As you go through the process of testing your idea, you build your knowledge of the domain you're working on, you develop your network and you start building a product. At each pivot, you use these assets to make an informed decision about the direction the company should take.

For example, you want to provide a better way for people to manage their mortgages. You soon find out, from speaking to potential customers, that managing mortgages isn't an issue. But customers did mention the purchasing process and what a pain it was. You then go and explore this issue.

This may seem logical, but many founders will give up on this process after the first three to four pivots. The best founders will persevere and build on their asset base, developing further niche knowledge and using the network they have already built to move fast.

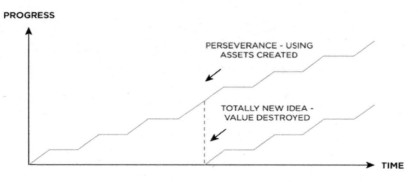

It's only through iteration and testing that you can get to a 'good' idea. But it also requires perseverance and a strong belief in your North Star.

Remember, customer development is there to inform your hunch, not to change your belief. Grant Aarons, co-founder of FabricNano, which seeks to replace all petrochemical products with bio-manufactured alternatives, said, 'It's a journey, and you need to stay in your path, you need to stay very focused on your vision and not let the world corrupt the vision of what you're trying to do as a company. That's the hardest part about being a founder.' The best founders we work with recognize when to pivot vs when to persevere.

Chapter Summary

Speaking to the customer is how founders illuminate insights that underpin the world's best startups.

- Seek out potential early adopters by homing in on people who have a 'hair on fire' problem.

- Listen in order to understand your customer's pain; don't set out to sell your idea.
- Don't get too attached to an idea, a design or a company. Do stay centred around your belief.
- Pivoting isn't always positive. Linear ideation ensures you don't destroy value every time you pivot.

PART 3

Growing and Scaling

No startup is an island. As a founder, you must understand the broader entrepreneurial ecosystem in which your company will be operating. In this section, we frame fundraising to help you get ahead of investor expectations and provide a primer on how to approach the seed round. Beyond that, we introduce you to others who can be helpful in your founding journey. Building a company from scratch can feel as isolating as it does invigorating, and at each new stage, you don't know what you don't know. Listening to the wrong people can be catastrophic, and forming a solid team of trusted mentors, coaches and advisors can be invaluable.

Growing into your role as a founder means scaling yourself. As you bring on more customers and build out your team, you must also hit your stride as an effective leader. We cover the dos and don'ts of establishing a high-performing culture that extends your vision and values to a team.

Lastly, we'll share how to differentiate between simply being busy and setting a successful trajectory. We left consulting more than a decade ago to explore a hunch, and the company we built now spans continents. We want you to achieve the same kind of staying power with your idea by using this practical advice for the road ahead.

CHAPTER 12

An Introduction to Startup Financing

Headlines in tech press publications like *TechCrunch* or *Wired* usually emphasize how much capital a company has raised. If a company has hit the 'unicorn' valuation of $1 billion, that's the headline. You might have the impression that the only thing that matters in the startup world is fundraising.

That's understandable – for a founder, a high valuation often feels like high validation. Most founders have a period where it feels like no one believes or even cares. So, when an investor shows up with a term sheet, it's usually an emotional high.

But fundraising is not the goal. It's a tool to help you get to your goal, reaching as many people as possible with your solution. Every time you raise venture capital, you're selling equity. Yes, you now have the funds to grow, but you own less of your company than you did before. Fundraising is full of trade-offs, and this chapter is designed to help you navigate them.

When we started Entrepreneur First, neither of us had met a venture investor before. We assumed the bar for getting a meeting with one – never mind actually raising money from them – must be impossibly high. The idea that there was a whole group of people whose job was to give entrepreneurs money seemed almost fantastical. If you're in the same position today as we were then, the good news is that not only do VCs exist, but there are more of them deploying more capital than ever before – and, in general, if you're building an ambitious company, they actively want to meet you.

But that doesn't mean that fundraising is easy – or even that it's the right path for most entrepreneurs. Before you take money from anyone, you want to make sure you understand *their* business model: What are their expectations? What do they want in return? You can fire employees. You can even fire your customers. You cannot fire your investors. One way or another, you're going to be in business with them until you either sell or leave the company. Understanding the range of financing options available to you – and picking the right one – is a critical step in your journey.

At EF, we've funded over 500 startups and been involved in financing rounds for companies worth well over a billion dollars. We've also raised hundreds of millions of dollars ourselves from some of the world's most respected investors. This chapter focuses on the types of funders you might encounter and delves into their motivations for investing. The following chapter outlines in more detail how to make sure you're building your business on solid financial foundations. Our focus in this book is on early-stage companies raising initial 'seed' rounds of funding. Although we may allude to Series A etc., we won't go into depth on each subsequent round.

Should You Fundraise?

One of the first questions founders should consider is whether they should seek outside funding at all. For many entrepreneurs, the best way to finance your company is through revenue. If you sell enough of a product or service to enough customers to generate profits, you can reinvest those profits in your business. Bootstrapping – funding the growth of your company entirely through revenue – provides two big advantages. First, it's non-dilutive. You don't give up any ownership when you sell a product; you do when you sell shares. Second, it pushes you to make something that your customer values from the beginning. It becomes painfully obvious if you're not making money because the company won't be able to pay your bills – or your team's pay cheques.

So, if it's so great, why doesn't everyone bootstrap? Most startups that plan to get big fast need external capital for three reasons.[16] One, many products take time to develop before customers are willing to pay for them. This is especially true if you're building something technically complex. If you're building something very tangible, you might be able to 'pre-sell' the product to potential customers using a platform like Kickstarter. But most of the time, funding the creation of a product that doesn't exist yet out of revenue isn't an option.

Two, the investments you want to make in growth – even if you do have revenue – are often larger than you can fund from day-to-day sales. One way of thinking about venture capital is that it allows your company to grow faster than your revenue. That's a choice, of course, but in some highly competitive markets – especially those with strong network effects or other 'first scaler advantages' – it's usually a venture-backed startup that wins.

You shouldn't elevate any particular source of financing to a goal in its own right. Just as there are some people who fetishize raising from VCs, there are others for whom bootstrapping is almost a religion. We think this is silly. Your financing strategy is a business decision like any other. Think carefully about your company's needs and choose accordingly.

If you're starting a company that can't provide revenue on Day One, or you need to grow faster than your revenue will allow, you need to look at external financing options. If you're not familiar with VC, you might think about getting a bank loan. But you almost certainly won't get one if you're building a high-risk, high-reward business. The economics simply don't work for a bank loan. Bankers know that most startups fail, so the interest they get from the successful companies wouldn't get close to making up for all the loans that go bad.

The solution for most startups is some sort of equity financing. This means that investors give you money in exchange for shares in your

---

[16] There are exceptions. In 2021, Intuit bought Mailchimp for $12bn. Mailchimp had never taken on external financing. But this is very rare.

business.[17] The attraction for these investors is that if your company becomes enormously successful, their upside is uncapped. Their shares could become worth ten, a hundred, or even a thousand times what they paid for them. We'll talk about the different types of equity investors and their business models in the next section.

When should you do this? The short answer is: when you can't reach your next important milestone without spending more money than is coming in. Sometimes that's close to the very beginning, if you need to go full-time to make progress and need a salary, for example. Other times you might be able to get a first version of your product in the hands of customers before you need to raise. In general, the earlier you need to raise, and the fewer proof points you have, the lower valuation investors are likely to ascribe to your business. Fortunately, as we'll discuss in the next section, there are lots of venture investors that are set up to invest from Day One.

One note before we get there, however: we strongly recommend that you raise money only from experienced, professional investors. For the world's best venture capitalists, investing in startups can be highly lucrative. For most people, it's an easy way to lose money. Most startups fail. When they do succeed, it takes many years with ups and downs along the way. There's no way to get your money out unless the startup sells. As an investor, you have almost no control over – or sometimes even visibility of – what happens along the way. These are hard lessons, and you *really* don't want to be on the receiving end of someone learning them for the first time.

This applies especially to people with whom you have a close personal relationship. It used to be common to talk about a startup's first financing as the 'friends and family round'. This always seemed bizarre to us. Quite apart from the fact that no one wants to sit down to a holiday meal across the table from a parent who's wondering what

---

[17] Or they give you money in exchange for the right to get shares in your business in the future. This is how common fundraising instruments like SAFEs (Simple Agreement for Future Equity) or convertible notes work. They have a slightly different legal structure, but ultimately, the investor wants the same thing – a stake in your business.

happened to their life savings, it suggests that if you didn't have friends and family with piles of cash lying around, startups weren't for you. Fortunately, there are many options today for financing your company that don't require a wealthy background or even a deep personal network.

Whatever you do, never take investment on an informal or 'back of a napkin' basis. Use an experienced lawyer who is familiar with startup investments and create a proper, binding agreement.

Picking the Investor Who's Right for You

Professional startup investors run the gamut from individuals who might invest as little as a few thousand dollars to huge institutions whose preferred cheque size is hundreds of millions. Whenever you raise money, you want to build a shortlist of investors whose investment size, stage and model is right for now. For the first round of financing, there are three main types of investors you might consider:

- **Accelerators, talent investors and incubators**: These organizations exist to help startups get going at the very earliest stage. They typically provide hands-on support as well as a small-ish amount of capital.
- **Angel investors**: These are wealthy individuals who invest in startups for a financial return (and sometimes for fun). They vary hugely in their approach and investment amount, but they typically invest early in a company's journey.
- **Venture capital firms**: These are institutions that are set up specifically to fund early-stage companies. Their business model requires them to focus on startups that can grow very quickly and become very large.

It's worth saying that raising capital is almost never a one-time thing. Most startups need multiple 'rounds' of funding, usually twelve to twenty-four months apart and with a significant increase in the amount of capital raised and the valuation each time. So you might well raise from an accelerator, a group of angel investors *and* a venture capital firm sequentially or simultaneously.

We'll run through each of these in more detail to give you a framework for deciding what's right for you. Keep in mind that you'll likely use a combination of these types of investors at different points in your entrepreneurial journey.

Accelerators and Talent Investors

The purpose of an accelerator is to help founders who have many of the core ingredients of a startup – a great team, a promising idea, maybe an initial version of the product – but haven't baked their idea enough to entice investors. The idea is that you enter an accelerator programme with these ingredients, and a few months later you emerge with a company that is ready to raise a seed round. An accelerator provides a small amount of cash, typically just enough to cover your costs for the duration of the programme, and a lot of support in the form of mentorship, advice, network and community. Accelerators usually run cohort-based programmes that last for a fixed duration. They typically culminate in a pitching event that kicks off the fundraising process.

Talent investing, the category of venture investing we pioneered at Entrepreneur First, takes this a step further. You apply to join a cohort as an individual before you have a company or even a team. You receive a stipend to cover your personal living costs for a short period during which you look for a co-founder from within the cohort and iterate on an idea. After this period, if you've formed a company, the talent investor has the option to invest and then provides accelerator-like support for an additional period, usually a few months, to prepare you to raise a seed round.

One of the most valuable (and sometimes underrated) things about an accelerator or talent investor is that you can simply apply for funding and support, usually through a simple online application form. You don't need a warm introduction or a strong existing network. In fact, most accelerators *want* to be the on-ramp into the startup ecosystem for founders who aren't already deeply connected. This is one thing that makes them an excellent starting point for many entrepreneurs.

Some of the world's most valuable startups took part in famous accelerators like Y Combinator. But most didn't. You should think of accelerators as a potentially valuable but very optional step of your journey. Not all accelerator and talent investors offer the same advantages. Entrepreneurs should evaluate any accelerator before applying. Perform basic due diligence to make sure that there's alignment between what they can provide and your goals by asking questions like:

- What are your most successful companies worth?
- What do your alumni say about you? Can we speak to some?
- What support do you provide, other than money?
- Who will I get advice from during the programme?
- What kinds of investors invest in the companies that come through your programme? How much do your graduates typically raise?
- Do you specialize in any types of technology or sectors?

Accelerators take a 5–12 per cent stake in your company, so you should be very careful about who you decide to work with. On the one hand, alumni of some of the best programmes often say that it was the best decision they ever made, despite the equity cost. A good programme can radically change your trajectory and put you on the path to global success. A mediocre one could be the most expensive equity you ever give away. Part of the challenge is that the best programmes are very selective. For example, our acceptance rate at Entrepreneur First is in the single-digit percentages. Beware programmes that seem easy to get into but don't provide much value.

The best reason to take part in an accelerator or talent investor programme is if you feel you need the support and the network they provide to get your company ready to raise a seed round. The best reason to skip an accelerator is if you don't. Accelerators are expensive because they're investing a lot more than cash; if all you need is cash, you may be better going straight to angel investors or VCs. We turn to them next.

Angel investing

Professional angel investors – wealthy individuals who are willing to write a personal cheque to a company – can be a great source of capital for entrepreneurs. The best ones are quick and easy to work with, provide advice and expertise beyond their money and have great networks to help you raise subsequent rounds of funding. What's more, because they're investing their own money, they can sometimes be interested in businesses that wouldn't be a good fit for VCs. (VCs have the added pressure of meeting their own investors' expectations; we outline in the next section what that means for entrepreneurs.) It's worth noting that angel investors vary widely in their approach, style and preferred investment size. At one extreme, some angels might like to invest a few thousand dollars at a time; at the other, some particularly wealthy individuals might write cheques of a million dollars or more.

Angels and VCs usually share similar goals: they want to make money! It's unlikely an angel will fund your company if they can't see a way to make a return of many multiples of their initial investment. But angels often have other motivations too. They want to invest in ideas they're passionate about and in founders they like and find fun to work with.

Of course, a founder should evaluate an angel's suitability through the lens of whether they're someone they want to be in business with for the long term. Evaluate them on the experience and network they can bring alongside an investment, as well as the level of engagement (communication frequency, advisory role) they expect in exchange. The best angel investors can have a truly transformational impact on your company, out of all proportion to their cheque size and ownership. An angel can be an incredible ambassador and accelerator for your company – or an albatross.

Bringing bad investors onboard can destroy the company – or at least your enjoyment of running it. An angel with an especially large stake, perhaps a devil in disguise, could end up having a veto over subsequent rounds of funding or an impact on who is willing to invest. It's rare, but we've seen it happen. Unfortunately, ecosystems of all sizes can support some toxic components. If they're going to have a significant stake or a board seat, it's totally reasonable to ask a prospective investor for references from founders they've invested in before.

One way to minimize the potential for problems down the line is to be clear about expectations in both directions, particularly about the angel's level of involvement. It's good practice to keep your investors up to date, usually through a regular email that transparently lays out the highlights and lowlights of the previous month. This helps you manage your investors and their expectations and also makes it much easier for them to help you if they know what's going on. You should have realistic expectations, too. Angel investors, even famous ones, rarely move the needle on your company's success – that's your job!

Venture Capital

The first thing to know about venture capital is that it's not suitable for over 99 per cent of companies. Venture capital is concerned with the tiny number of companies that have the aspiration and the potential to become enormous. Fewer than one in 200 new companies raise from VC firms, but around half of those that successfully IPO (initial public offering) have done so – and seven of the eight most valuable companies in the world did.[18]

---

[18] Lerner, Josh, and Ramana Nanda. 'Venture Capital's Role in Financing Innovation: What We Know and How Much We Still Need to Learn'. *Journal of Economic Perspectives* 34, no. 3 (August 2020): 237–61. https://doi.org/10.1257/jep.34.3.237.

If you aspire to raise from VCs, it's important to understand the VC worldview. Unless you do, much of the way that VCs behave and the decisions they make can seem odd. As a business, VC is very simple. People who want to start a VC have to go and raise capital from other investors, who are called limited partners (LPs). LPs are typically institutions that manage large pools of capital and invest in VC alongside other asset classes such as the public stock market, bonds and real estate to diversify their portfolio.

There are lots of downsides to VC from an LP perspective. It's high risk, it's illiquid (i.e., you can't get your money out quickly as you can in the public stock markets), and it can take a very long time. So, in return for accepting these disadvantages, LPs have very high returns expectations – they want to see VCs return at least three times the money invested in a seven- to ten-year period. The very best funds do much better; it's not unheard of for a venture fund to return twenty times the original capital or more. Perhaps this sounds simple, but getting to this sort of return requires some brutal arithmetic that every entrepreneur should understand.

Imagine two people set out to be venture capitalists. They successfully persuade big pools of capital (such as pension funds, foundations, endowments, wealthy families, sovereign wealth funds or occasionally corporates) to invest $50 million in their seed fund. First hurdle cleared (and this is actually extremely challenging, especially for first-time VCs). How much money do they have to make to meet their LPs' expectations? Well, we mentioned that LPs want to see three times ('3x') their initial investment returned. But the VC business model is to charge LPs a 2 per cent management fee every year, plus 20 per cent of the profits. So, to comfortably clear 3x, the VC's investments need to be worth around 4x the original amount invested.

Let's say that the VCs' plan that, of the $50 million, they'll do twenty-five investments of $1 million in each startup. They will then reserve the rest of the capital to invest in later rounds of funding. (Almost all startups require multiple rounds of funding, so if the VCs don't reserve capital to follow on, their ownership will get diluted in the same way as the founders'.) Essentially, they've got twenty-five shots on goal. So, how big do they need each company to be to score?

Remember, we've just said that they are going to need to get four times the *whole fund* to make their LPs happy. That means that the fund needs to find $200 million of outcomes out of those twenty-five companies. But as we've said, it doesn't own 100 per cent of the companies. In a high valuation ecosystem like London, their initial $1 million might buy them 10 per cent ownership. The follow-on investing protects them from dilution a little, but even so, they won't have the capital to invest in all the later rounds – so, let's assume that they own 5 per cent at exit. The $200 million they need will represent just 5 per cent of the total exit value of the companies they invest in – in other words, they need the portfolio to be worth $4 *billion* to get to their target return.

Hopefully, they don't have just one winner out of twenty-five investments, but, equally, you're unlikely to have more than a couple of home runs. In a venture portfolio, the biggest company is usually bigger than all the rest put together, which means that in this case, the biggest company probably needs to be worth $2 billion for it to be a good fund. But, of course, the VC doesn't know which of the twenty-five will be the biggest at the point of the investment – if they did, it would be a very easy job! This means the VC needs to see a path for *each* investment being worth $2 billion, otherwise they will probably pass on the round.

When you start to think about this, it can seem a little crazy. The VC is being asked to invest at a $10 million valuation, but unless they can see a path to a multi-billion-dollar outcome, they're not interested? You can change the numbers a bit – maybe the initial valuation is a little lower, maybe the ultimate dilution is a little less – but the arithmetic remains brutal: VC only really works for companies that can quite plausibly be worth over a billion dollars.

Entrepreneurs are often surprised by how little alignment there is between a great outcome for a founder and a great outcome for a VC. If you start a relationship with a VC with the idea that selling the business for $100 million is great, you're right – for you. Even if you only own 20 per cent of that company when it sells, you'll never have to work again. For the VC, however, getting an offer of $100 million can be extremely frustrating. If this is a company they really believe in – one they were counting on to make a serious dent in their fund's returns target – they've essentially missed one of their shots on goal. You might want to take the offer, but your VC is much less likely to be excited. Your VC may even have the legal power – that's how these contracts work – to block that deal. In practice, if you're absolutely determined to take the offer, they probably won't refuse to sign. But it won't be a lot of fun.

Does that mean that once you're on the VC treadmill, it's double or quits for the founder all the way to an IPO or failure? That used to be relatively common, but today, secondary sales – which offer the founder an opportunity to cash out some of their equity as part of a fundraising round – are becoming more common at Series B or beyond. At that point, the company is becoming well established and de-risked. More importantly, from a VC's perspective, if you can take *some* cash out now – enough to stop you worrying about money day-to-day but not so much that you can buy an island – you're much less likely to want to take the next acquisition offer that comes your way. If an acquisition won't move the needle on your quality of life, you're much more aligned with the VC.

So, what kinds of companies *can* reach the bar for raising VC investment? Typically, they need four characteristics:

1. The company needs to be entering an enormous market – enough to support achieving hundreds of millions of dollars of revenue.
2. It needs to be able to grow very quickly so that they can reach an exit during the ten-year life of the VC fund.

3. Its business model needs to get better with scale. Ideally, it has high upfront fixed costs and then low marginal costs on each unit of product sold.

4. Its position within the market needs to be differentiated and defensible (for instance, patented technologies and rare skill sets) so that it doesn't get rapidly supplanted by competition. This is where network effects are very valuable.

Based on our experience, software companies are as close to a perfect business model as the world has seen. They often meet all four of these criteria – which is why most VC dollars go into software companies. You can try – and some people do – to raise VC for a non-software company, but it's like playing the game on 'really, really hard mode'.

All this said, we should emphasize that we're not anti-VC. In fact, we are VCs! For the right kind of company, venture capital can be a wonderful thing. As well as providing capital, the best VCs are highly experienced company builders who can help with strategic advice, hiring, later rounds of fundraising and negotiating a sale or IPO. We've been lucky enough at Entrepreneur First to work with some of the very best VCs in the world. As long as you know what you're getting into, and you choose the right partner, VCs can be a hugely valuable part of your success. So how do you choose a VC? What should you look for? That's our focus in the next chapter.

A Quick Note on Crowdfunding

Lots of founders ask us about crowdfunding. One possible exception to our rule of raising only from professional investors is raising money from a well-established and regulated crowdfunding platform – WeFunder or SeedInvest in the US, Crowdcube or Seedrs in the UK or Crowdtivate in Singapore. These platforms allow ordinary members of the public to invest in startups. They require all investors to explicitly acknowledge the risks involved and the fact that they won't have any right to get involved in the business. They also provide a robust legal investment agreement that protects you and the investors. Usually, this legal structure means you don't have to deal with dozens or even hundreds of shareholders directly. This model can work well for certain types of companies, especially those with highly engaged customer bases who would like to express their support by investing. Given that this group is now financially incentivized by your success, they are more likely to support you than a typical customer. Some very well-known startups, including fintech giants Revolut and Monzo, raised money through crowdfunding. Crowdfunding can be a useful part of your fundraising strategy, but in our experience, it's definitely not a magic bullet.

Chapter Summary

Fundraising is a tool, not an end. Knowing what drives different kinds of investors helps founders understand expectations.

- There are many ways to fund a business, but venture capital tends to be the best approach for ambitious startups that want to scale fast.
- There is great variation in priorities and style, even among experienced, professional investors.
- What seems like a fantastic deal for an entrepreneur might read as a huge disappointment to an investor – and vice versa.

CHAPTER 13

How to Raise Money

This chapter is not designed to be a comprehensive guide to raising a seed round from start to finish. That would require a whole book in itself – and there are some excellent ones that we'll point you to that already exist. Instead, we'll try to give you a general framework for thinking about raising capital and choosing the right partner for you.

How to Think About Fundraising

If you've never raised capital before, it can be easy to assume that VCs are hyper-rational calculating machines who build discounted cash flow models of your company and carefully make their decisions based on a first-principles deductive process. In our experience, early-stage fundraising is nothing like this. In fact, it can be highly irrational. Decisions are made:

1. by humans;
2. based on imperfect information;
3. in a constantly changing environment.

Some founders find this highly frustrating, which is understandable. Why can some companies you read about in Techcrunch raise $5 million with apparently little more than a deck while you're struggling to get any interest at all in your more modest round? Trying to come up with a rational answer to this will drive you crazy. Even the best investors sometimes make decisions based on non-rational factors – FOMO (fear of missing out), herd mentality, extrapolation from limited data points and even good old fashioned 'irrational exuberance'. Don't bother trying to make sense of early-stage valuations, and don't take it personally if an investor passes. The best you can do is research potential investors thoroughly, understand your investor's business model and motivations, calculate your company's cash needs and practise your pitch. In the following pages, we've outlined a few ways to think about your approach to fundraising to help you prepare.

Scenario Planning

It's very easy to see fundraising as the goal, but keep in mind that capital is just a tool. Optimize for the business you're trying to build, not for the fundraising. That's where scenario planning comes in. Before you set out to raise money, founding teams should have clear answers to the following questions:

- **What are the milestones that we need to raise the *next* fund round?** This might seem a little odd as you've not raised *this* round yet. But it's a helpful way for investors to understand if you're aligned in your plans and ambitions – and to sense check your growth and planning assumptions. Usually, we think about this in terms of the milestones needed to raise the next round of funding, as few startups will be profitable after the seed round. For example, for a lot of software companies, you need to reach around $1m of annual recurring revenue (ARR) and still be growing fast (say at least 10 per cent a month) to raise a Series A. These milestones will vary for different types of companies. For example, consumer companies that might monetize later might be evaluated more in terms of usage, engagement and retention. Deep tech companies might need to demonstrate that they've cracked a key technical milestone and have proof of demand from the likely eventual customers. In all cases, the question is something like: What does 'product-market fit' look like for you?

- **How much do we need to raise to achieve these?** What is the absolute minimum needed to meet these milestones? How much more could we do or how much quicker could we go if we had more capital? Typically, startups raise between twelve- and twenty-four-months' worth of expenses – known as 'runway' – to take the business to the next stage.

- **What will we spend the money on?** In particular, who do we need to hire and how quickly? When can we realistically expect these people to start work, and how long do they need to start having the desired impact?

We encourage entrepreneurs to map out several possible futures. Identify your Plan A, the ideal scenario; a Plan B, launching with less; and a Plan Z, which answers the question: *What if everyone says no? What would you do if you couldn't raise money for another six months? Is there any path forward?* (Entrepreneurs are perennially optimistic. It might be sensible to add a buffer of anywhere from 20 per cent to 50 per cent to your best-case budget projections.)

These are not easy questions to answer, particularly if you've not worked in or around startups before. This is one of the areas where a good accelerator or experienced mentor will be able to help. In fact, most accelerators see having their graduates raise a good seed round as their most important performance indicator.

Principles for Successful Seed Raises

Entire books have been written on fundraising strategy, from planning to pitching, negotiating to closing. We recommend *The Fundraising Field Guide* by Carlos Espinal, Managing Partner at Seedcamp, one of the most successful seed funds in Europe. In his book, Espinal offers founders in-depth insights into the fundraising challenges and process for high-growth, early-stage tech startups.

We're not going to get into detailed tactical or process advice here, but we do want to share our golden principles that will serve you well as you raise a seed round, whatever your business.

- **Seed is about people.** At this stage, you won't have a lot of revenue or other concrete metrics, so above all, the investor is backing you. That means that you do need to seem like a formidable founder, but you also need to seem like someone the investor will want to work with for a long time.
- **Project a vision.** As we emphasized in the last chapter, one of the most important things for a VC is believing that your company can be huge. Today it is tiny, so your ability to tell a story about how and why it can grow many orders of magnitude is critical.
- **Fundraising is sales – and so is everything else.** As a CEO, most of what you do is sales: getting a customer over the line, persuading a key hire to join you, signing a big partnership. Investors want to know that you can sell – and one good test is whether you can sell to *them*. You need to be authentic, of course, but there's no doubt that one of the things that investors are looking for is raw persuasive power.
- **Answer the question.** A rambling, unclear or confusing response can tank the investor's first impression of you. Give full, direct answers. Preparing crisp, clear answers to the most likely questions gives you a big advantage.
- **Tell stories.** Use stories and anecdotes to bring your company to life, especially when explaining something complex that a generalist investor may not be familiar with. Stories about customers can convey insight and empathy that can make your business much easier to understand.
- **Know your numbers.** Unit economics. Conversion rates. Competitor market share. If you've got numbers in your presentation, make sure you know where they came from and what they mean. There are no excuses for being sloppy on numbers.

- **Strong beliefs weakly held.** Investors are looking for confidence and conviction, but also someone who listens and responds to new information. You don't need to be defensive if an investor asks something challenging or questions one of your assumptions; use it as an opportunity to explain *why* you've made the business decisions you have.
- **Surprise them.** Share some unexpected insight into how your industry works or emerging customer behaviour. Investors love meetings where they walk away having learnt something.

Choosing a Partner

Founders often feel like investors have all the power. But as soon as you get a term sheet (an investment offer that summarizes the key terms), it can feel like the tables turn rapidly, particularly if you're fortunate enough to get more than one. How should you choose between competing investment offers?

We tell founders that there are four major things you should take into consideration: terms, support, brand and relationship.

Terms

Valuation is probably the first thing most founders think of when deciding how to choose between offers. And all other things equal, higher is better – it's the price at which you're selling your equity, and (hopefully) you think your equity is very valuable. But it's not the only important thing. As long as you're raising enough money to reach your goals, you should care about dilution – how much your ownership percentage will reduce as a result of the round – as much as valuation. Imagine two offers: one to invest $1.5m at a $6m valuation and one to invest $4m at a $9m valuation. Which is better? It depends. If you don't need the extra money now to get to your next milestone (and so have the chance of raising substantially more money at an even higher valuation), it might be better to take the lower offer – which results in

20 per cent dilution – than the apparently higher one, which results in around 30 per cent dilution.[19]

One thing we would emphasize is that many first-time founders underrate the value of speed relative to valuation. If you have a decent offer now from someone you like and believe can help, you have to decide whether it's worth spending several more weeks – or even months – to meet other investors in hopes of maximizing your valuation. In our experience, it's usually not. Moving at speed in the early stages of your company is absolutely critical to success. Gaining a couple of percentage points of ownership at the cost of six weeks of founder bandwidth is very rarely worth it.

You should also be aware that some of the less obvious terms you might see in an investment offer can significantly alter its attractiveness. We highly recommend Brad Feld and Jason Mendelson's book *Venture Deals,* which walks through these in a lot of detail. You can also find an example termsheet at howtobeafounder.com.

Support

Almost every venture capital firm claims to offer support beyond the money. That varies from a single partner taking a board seat through to firms like Andreessen Horowitz, which have literally hundreds of staff to help with everything from sales and marketing to human resources.

Investors *can* be transformational for a company. Investors can advise. Investors can connect. But they can't do the work for you. Founders are still responsible for building the company. It's important to calibrate expectations accordingly. Think of investors not as fairy godmothers who will come and wave a magic wand to fix your problems, but as champions who can amplify successes and be a rock in a crisis.

Good VCs are experts in company building. They will not understand the intricacies of your company as well as you do, but there is a lot of pattern recognition around the core challenges of maturing a startup.

---

[19] We calculate this as $1.5m / ($1.5m + $6m) = 20\%$ and $4m / ($4m + $9m) = 30.7\%$

Don't be afraid to ask what your prospective investors see as their core areas of expertise and network strength. If they seem to be promising a lot, ask for concrete examples of how they've had an impact on portfolio companies in the past.

And as common as it is for investors to claim that they're more than cash, it's sometimes quite refreshing when they don't. For instance, Tiger Global – an American investment firm – has gained prominence by taking a different tack. Their pitch is essentially, 'We don't help. That's not what we're here for. We'll be cheaper and faster than anyone else.' A lot of entrepreneurs love this. When Tiger says, 'We don't help,' founders hear, 'We don't meddle.' You ask founders what they want – they want speed, price and autonomy. Tiger figured out a way to give all three.

That may or may not be right for you – it depends on your level of experience and the nature of the challenges your company faces. Think hard about what you need to get to the next stage and use this as one input for your choice of investor.

Brand

Investor brand is a big driver of founder decision-making. Faced with offers from Sequoia Capital – perhaps the world's most successful VC, which backed Google, Airbnb, Stripe and many others at the earliest stage – and a new no-name fund, picking Sequoia is a no-brainer for most entrepreneurs. That's not irrational. Raising from a top brand does have benefits for a company. It can open doors with candidates (particularly executive hires), later-stage investors and even customers. The networks of the most celebrated firms are usually extraordinary.

But it's important not to let the brand of your investor become a vanity metric. Ultimately, you'll succeed because of the company you build, not because you have famous backers. Causality probably flows in the opposite direction – great companies attract the best VCs because they're already great; they don't become great because they have the best VCs. There's nothing wrong with wanting to pitch the top brands.

But exercise caution. Sometimes famous funds, especially the very large ones, might offer a small cheque to a startup that's one or two stages earlier than the fund's core focus. It can be very tempting to take this over an offer from a smaller or newer fund – but if you're not going to move the needle for the big fund, you may not see any benefits. It's often better to be a big deal to a smaller fund than a minnow to a bigger one.

Relationship

Money is often raised in a hurry. But you could be getting into a ten-year relationship with someone after a process that's taken a few weeks if you're lucky. Think about how much emphasis we put on testing the co-founder relationship. You're not going to spend as many hours in the day with your investor, but you will be tied together long-term. It's important to figure out if you're aligned on values and mission. For us, our closest investors are people we speak to sometimes weekly and certainly monthly. You don't want to take those calls or meetings with dread. These people are going to exercise a lot of influence on what the company becomes – resisting them is going to take a lot of your mental energy and headspace that would be better directed at solving your business problems. Make sure that you're broadly gunning for the same goals, not just financially, but in terms of culture, values and mission.

Despite its salience in startup culture, raising capital is not the goal. It is a milestone, but it's only the fuel that you use to do the next step of the journey. Fundraising is a skill – and an important one. But in the end, it's a relatively small part of a founder's job. No amount of fundraising success will make up for a lack of product-market fit or poor execution. In some ways, the core job of a founder becomes harder once you have a lot of money in the bank – there are a lot more ways to mess up! Your journey is just beginning, and you're almost certainly going to want a lot more help along the way. That's what we turn to next.

Chapter Summary

Even when raising a seed round, savvy founders need to think a few steps ahead:

- Map out multiple scenarios for how your company will use varying levels of support to achieve maximum growth.
- Dilution is just as important a consideration as valuation.
- Recognize that working with an investor is a long-term relationship, and consider holistically the value of the relationship and the values they bring to the table.

CHAPTER 14

Preparing for the Road Ahead

If you choose this path, you will embark on the steepest learning curve of your life, a curve that is often very lonely and poorly understood by others. You won't collect the same badges as your family and friends, and they probably won't understand what you're attempting to do. Most days, neither will you. There are very few other careers that allow you to go on such an unconstrained personal growth journey. Even if you read this book many times over, you will underestimate the difficulty of your endeavour until you truly begin.

Luckily, there are others who have navigated the journey ahead of you and will prove to be invaluable. Founder stereotypes create a false image of startup leaders as superhero geniuses who go it all alone and seem to have all the answers. They know exactly where they're going and land one piece of flawless execution after the other. In reality, there will be many moments of uncertainty. As a founder, you will need to know where to turn when you lack clarity or competence in an area. You will, of course, be in constant dialogue with your co-founder, but don't underrate trusted people outside the company whom you can approach for advice.

In our experience developing hundreds of successful entrepreneurs, the best founders are usually those who have the most questions. They are the most open and honest about what they don't know and where they need help. For the startup founder, help can come from a variety of sources. Typically, these people are classified as mentors, advisors, coaches or board members. It's important to understand what you can ask of each and what they typically expect in return. Some engagements are rooted in a finite project or specific problem, and others can be ongoing relationships that deeply influence the enterprise strategy.

Mentors

Mentorship is an overused umbrella term with an almost mystical allure. When you see a mentorship relationship working, it looks great, and new entrepreneurs tend to try to replicate the outcome. First-time founders run around searching for someone successful to take them under their wing – a guru who will guide them every step of the journey. But long-term, mutually enriching mentorship relationships typically don't start by asking, 'Will you be my mentor?' or even with the general request to pick someone's brain over coffee. When you take this approach, you are focusing on what you *imagine* you want your relationship to be rather than what you actually need from it. Sheryl Sandberg raises this challenge in *Lean In*, where she observes how often total strangers are asked to become mentors. 'The strongest [mentor] relationships spring out of a real and often earned connection felt by both sides,' she said.

Strong relationships are the result of a period of interactions between two people where one has a problem and the other one knows how to solve it. Think of it from the position of the person on the other side of the table. In general, almost no one on the mentor side is looking to take a stranger under their wing. Yes, it's intrinsically satisfying to pass on hard-won knowledge and experience to help people succeed. But picking a fundraising expert's brain on scaling an engineering team is painful to the mentor and probably not very helpful to you. The best way for a mentor to contribute and feel satisfied is by sharing insights on topics for which they feel genuine excitement and mastery.

We define a mentor as someone who can help you with a specific subject matter or functional expertise. They have experience, so their advice is validated and will be directly helpful to your organization. They typically aren't formally retained or given equity in the company, but they're willing to share their knowledge as an act of goodwill to build a stronger startup ecosystem.

Say you've just hit product-market fit. Suddenly, you need to figure out how to scale a sales team to serve more customers. If you need a sales mentor, then you need to find someone who has scaled an enterprise sales team to offer tactical advice and walk you through the professional capacities you need to build. A good mentor for an early-stage founder is often a startup founder who is two years ahead of them on a similar journey – someone like Elon Musk doesn't remember what it was like to have your problems. The right mentor will have granular experience and be able to help you understand how to move through this problem.

People underestimate the power of peer mentorship. More seasoned founders can be great, too, but the startup landscape is always rapidly evolving. How do you raise a seed round? How do you hire your first exec? The knowledge they have is fresh and relevant.

A subject-matter mentor might become someone who you repeatedly seek out. If, over time, the same person turns out to be a valuable source of advice on a series of functional and technical topics, the relationship that develops is special. The point is not to aim for that relationship but for the value that you get along the way – partly because that's the only way it can be valuable for the mentor. It enriches both people's lives and their work. Having been on both sides of the table, we can say that, as a mentor, there is nothing more satisfying than truly wishing for (and seeing) the success of someone that you've helped.

By thinking about mentors in this way, you will likely find many who have a wide variety of experiences, but if you get frequent advice from someone who turns out to be instrumental to the success of your company, offering them a more formal role in the company as an advisor and/or a small piece of equity might be merited. Because if things work out, it's good to formally acknowledge the people who helped you along the way.

Coaches

Coaching is different from mentoring but often conflated. Mentors must be experienced subject-matter experts in ways a coach does not have to be. A coach is good at helping you analyse and improve *your* performance. They need to know how to ask the right questions. They need to know how to direct your attention to the right places, and they need to know how to help you help yourself. A coach can't tell you how to run your company. That's not what they're there for. But they can help you confront difficult questions about yourself, the situation you're in, your relationships, and pinpoint other things that might be holding you back. Their job is to unlock the best version of you.

We see this all the time in the sports domain. Serena Williams has had a coach throughout her career. Williams's coach is definitely not a better tennis player than her, but he knew how to ask questions and run drills that would push his players to improve. Many of us have been coached in sports at some point and will talk openly about how we benefited from that experience. We're seeing a shift toward embracing coaching, not as a remedial measure to correct bad executive behaviour but as a proactive performance enhancer. Engaging a leadership coach or executive coach creates the space in which you can address the biggest challenges to your performance, but it will also challenge the way you think about yourself (which is necessary, but not always easy).

Almost always, coaches should be paid cash for services. You don't want your coach to have skin in the game. You want to be able to tell them, 'I think I'm about to trash this company down to zero,' without seeing them flinch in distress. If you want to learn more about what good coaches look like, we recommend the book *Trillion Dollar Coach: The Leadership Playbook of Silicon Valley's Bill Campbell*. Co-authored by Alan Eagle, Eric Schmidt and Jonathan Rosenberg, it outlines how Campbell played an instrumental coaching role in the growth of startup giants such as Google, Apple and Intuit. 'A coach is someone who tells you what you don't want to hear, who has you see what you don't want to see, so you can be who you've always known you can be,' said Landry, who coached the Dallas Cowboys through twenty straight winning seasons and two Superbowl Titles.

In the book, Eagle, Schmidt and Rosenberg highlight coachability as a key indicator for success. Traits of a coachable entrepreneur include honesty and humility because a successful coaching relationship requires a great degree of vulnerability.

Advisors

Advisors can bring credibility, contacts and advice to your business. This role is a formally contracted relationship between a startup and someone with a specific area of expertise or experience who plans to be formally involved in the business. The advisor typically has some upside; they're incentivized based on the overall success of the company, particularly at an early stage that is paid as equity in your company. The scope of expertise you will call on from an advisor is usually more open-ended around enterprise strategy than the functional expertise of a mentor. As a door-opener, advisors can reach out to their networks with warm introductions.

Advisors can also lend credibility to your company. Medical technology startups will take on eminent doctors as advisors early on to demonstrate legitimacy, for example. However, be careful about borrowing credibility through advisor equity. We caution against offering equity to a subject matter expert in exchange for what is essentially a book jacket blurb. Carefully consider whether their credibility transfers to you and how involved they plan to be. Critically examine whether this person is excited about what you're doing and wants to engage with your challenges. At some point, a potential investor or the press will call them up and ask them what they think of you. If they can't remember who you are, it's not gonna work (and will look terrible!). It's much better to build authentic relationships with champions who truly believe in you than to buy credibility.

Advisors can help you to avoid pitfalls/wrong turns and pressure test your decisions. The best advice will often feel challenging and sometimes uncomfortable. It can be tactical, too.

'In my experience, at the earliest stages of a business most entrepreneurs prefer advisors who provide actionable advice rather than coaching,' said Chris Mairs, advisor to some of Europe's most successful startups. 'A coach might ask, "Have you thought about why your revenue forecasts are so wrong?" In contrast, actionable advice might be, "It's usually worth managing your sales funnel quite closely with timelines, contract values and weighted probabilities of closing. Let me send you a couple of examples that I have seen work in the past which you might want to adapt."'

Board Members

Founders tend to want to avoid having a board because they think their board will 'get in the way' or slow them down. At EF, we have seen that it's generally helpful to have a board.

Having a board creates a cadence of accountability. You have to give them accurate information on a consistent basis, even if things are dropping or dipping. Any board member worth their salt knows that startups are hard and things are going to go wrong. Board members with experience won't be freaked out when they do. As long as you are updating your board – honestly and openly keeping them in the loop – it's hard to blindside them. If you do have a challenge that isn't expected, your board members know what's happened, and they often become your biggest supporters in those difficult times. Ideally, look for potential board members with multiple experiences in different early-stage startups who are willing to take the journey with you.

Having board members whose job it is to think differently, challenge and support you helps prevent self-deception. One of the greatest risks for founders is kidding yourself. Self-deception is especially attractive when things aren't going well. When things get hard, founders tend to ask the wrong questions or get stuck on the hard bit and lose sight of the rest of their goals. A good board member can get you back on track and in pursuit of answers to the right question.

If you're going to create a board at seed, it should include the people who are most aligned with your goal to get the company to the next stage. This includes investors. However, we don't generally advise that you pay investors as board members. If they're taking a seat on the board as part of the funding round, that's essentially their job. Their remuneration comes in the form of shares in your company.

As you grow, it can be helpful to have independent subject matter or industry experts on board. You're going to want a small group of people who, when you have to make major decisions, can be there to represent expertise or perspectives that are different from your own. The key is to be open to their perspectives, even if you disagree with them, or their feedback might kill your idea. That requires mutual trust and transparency. If you can cultivate those qualities with your board, then they can provide that extra layer of resilience to help you win.

Few things are more valuable than a board member who truly believes in you. Who, regardless of what today's data shows, sees the long-term potential in your company even when you're feeling unsure? As co-founders, your moods are typically in sync. If times are hard in the company, you're both down. If the company is growing well, you're both floating on cloud nine. But having a board member who really believes and buys into the thesis gives you 'counter-cyclical resilience'. They can keep you on track when things feel good by being a little more grounded. And when you and your co-founder are both really down, they can remind you why they (and you!) are excited about the startup.

Chapter Summary

Founders should build trusting relationships with experienced entrepreneurs and investors who can share their wisdom and offer encouragement along the journey.

- Mentors, coaches, advisors and board members each play varying roles with different relationships to you and your company.
- Cultivate a mix of people who challenge you, hold you accountable, have recent experience and have a mature outlook on the entrepreneurial ecosystem.

CHAPTER 15

Building Culture

We often say, 'Culture is the third co-founder.' If starting a startup is the ultimate source of leverage in a career, culture is the ultimate source of leverage within a startup. 'Culture is infrastructure for scale,' says Christa Davies, CFO at Aon and board member at Stripe and Workday. There comes a point, quite rapidly, where the founders can't do everything themselves and need to hire people. Of course, you want everyone you hire to be talented and diligent, but it's your culture that will determine how effective they are as a team. 'You have to think about it from the beginning,' said Sara Clemens, COO Twitch and angel investor. 'Culture is easy to establish and hard to change.'

It's a little bit like an accent – you recognize when others have one but can't always hear your own. Although culture doesn't begin to create significant leverage until after the product and team take off, you set its foundations from the very beginning, consciously or not. When it's just you and your co-founder, the way you work together *is* the culture. Even if you're not at all deliberate about it, the way you work will embody the preferences, norms, ideals and values of the founders – and anyone who joins you will start to sense, imitate and replicate them. This is culture.

One way of thinking about the goal of a company culture is that it should nudge people to make decisions and behave as you'd want them to if you were in the room. Early on, you often *will* be in the room, but as your company scales, you become a smaller and smaller part of the everyday operations. At the start, you and your co-founder share the workload, debating every decision and personally setting each directive. With rapid growth, things change very quickly. The team outgrows the table, and the 'everyone does everything' model becomes impossible.

Of course, we're not saying that in all successful companies, everyone is a clone of the founders and would do whatever the founders do in every situation. It's a big advantage to have teammates with diversity of thought and skill sets. But having a distinct culture ensures that your team understands the vision, mission and values that you want to underpin everything you do as a company. As a founder, there's nothing more jarring than hearing about something your company has done or said that feels counter to your values or purpose. But it's almost inevitable as you scale – and a strong culture is the antidote.

A strong culture minimizes the number of decisions you need to make as a founder. This is a good thing. If you were needed in every meeting, if you had to weigh in on every choice, you're almost certainly not going to build a scalable company. If your culture guides the company towards the decisions you'd make without you having to be there, you have more time to focus on the highest-impact activity. **Culture is leverage**.

Finally, culture is a competitive advantage when it comes to building your team. Great people want to work in companies with great cultures. Your culture should create a sense of meaning, autonomy and impact.

Intentionally Building a Culture

As soon as you add another person to your team, they will absorb what they see in their leaders. Founders set the tone and direction of the culture with everything they do. You can't come up with it in an afternoon, slap it on the wall and hope that it sticks. Articulating values is useful because it helps you communicate, but it doesn't change who you are and how you behave. In the earliest stages of your organization, you need to live your values, not just print them.

A good way to think about intentionally building culture is to think about the critical actions that founders take that crystallize a culture. There are many, but we want to highlight some that are particularly important: what you praise; what you say (and show) is important; how you deal with poor performance; how you deal with setbacks; and how you deal with challenge and criticism. Let's look at these in turn.

One of the most important determinants of culture is what founders praise. In a good startup, people will admire and respect the founders. Praise is currency, so people will (consciously or otherwise) adapt their behaviour to earn it. If founders praise the wrong things, people read the wrong signals about what's important. A common cultural mistake is excessive praise for outcomes rather than process. Of course, you want great outcomes. But founders must recognize that the outcome itself is not the focus – you want more of the *behaviour* that causes the outcome. Praising outcomes privileges the endpoint while failing to recognize a chain of activities that led to the outcome. For instance, if you praise the sale, you miss out on the product marketing that made the sale possible. If your culture celebrates moments of completion, your best people are going to gravitate to that action. Now, that might be right for your business. But if you're not careful, you create a very transactional culture where people compete to be recognized for crossing the finish line rather than for the full process that creates value on the way.

People pay close attention to what the founders find important and how they demonstrate it. What gets celebrated and how? Are you writing notes of appreciation, taking staff out for dinner, or offering a company-wide shoutout on Slack? When more funding comes in, where is it spent? How do the founders talk about money? Do they celebrate wins with conspicuous consumption or demonstrate frugality? There's no 'right' answer, but you should be aware that even seemingly personal choices impact how people think and behave. Humans are adept at reading the signals of what it takes to fit in somewhere. That's why culture is so powerful. When you hire someone, you're getting their skill set, experience and know-how, but their behaviours will converge rapidly on whatever is 'normal' in your company.

Founders shape culture by how they deal with mistakes and poor performance. In some cultures, a manager will publicly take an employee down for a mistake. 'You cost us that sale. If you don't shape up, you're out of here. What's wrong with you?' In other cultures, the same mistake would be quietly ignored. Probably neither approach is healthy – each leads to a different type of dysfunction. The range of what's considered normal in managing conflict is wide, and you need to be clear about what you want to see in your organization.

When a company has setbacks, the founders' response is crucial. What that response is – or whether there is silence around the issue – will shape the culture. If founders aren't transparent about problems, they build a culture where what leaders say has no bearing on how the company is actually performing. You build low levels of trust. If the norm in your organization is to sweep failure under the carpet, they will sweep it under the carpet – and you won't know when things are starting to go wrong until it's too late.

How do founders handle it when an employee challenges them? Are people allowed to say, 'You told us we're going to do this, but we haven't done it. Why is that?' Or are the founders treated like quasi-religious figures who have to be praised? It's nice to feel admired and respected, but if you create barriers to people telling you what's really going on or how they really feel, you'll be much slower to receive and respond to crucial information. How you and your co-founder model giving and receiving feedback, and whether you engage in candid, robust conversations, will set the tone for how the team treats you.

If you're unsure what kind of culture you've built, ask your team to describe the principles, standards and behaviours they already see. It's a revealing exercise. They're much more likely to have an accurate view of your culture than you are. If you do the exercise and feel it's not what you hoped to hear, think about what needs to change to get to the place you want to be. It's not enough to plaster your values all over the office; it's your own actions and behaviour that will drive change. Articulating values works only if they map to the reality everyone experiences. If they don't, it's not just useless – it's corrosive.

The words on the wall at Entrepreneur First? *Be the team that founders want to work with.* In other words, founders first. Customer first. That phrase articulates our aspiration for our team. But if we as co-founders don't live it, it doesn't matter how bold and large the typeface. It's not what we'll see. Emphasizing the customers – in our case, entrepreneurs – we work with and for keeps us aligned and accountable to our mission. Without that, it's impossible to succeed at scale.

Common Mistakes Founders Make in Building Culture

When we speak to founders who have a culture problem in the organization, they're typically taken by surprise – particularly during periods of rapid scale or when the founders are focused on fundraising and distracted from the core business.

Maybe you come back into the office after being out for meetings for a week or so. You notice something is off and wonder, 'Huh, when did this start?' If you have multiple teams, you might notice a shift from a cooperative attitude to 'us versus them'. You might think that you had nothing to do with creating that dynamic. But there was likely a moment when you took a shortcut or didn't challenge a borderline behaviour and, quite insidiously, new norms started to kick in. As a founder, you not only have to pay close attention to symptoms of toxicity, but you have to be constantly vigilant that your own behaviour isn't promoting it, however unintentionally. If you act passively and don't call out behaviours that you don't like, or if you don't praise behaviours that you do like, then the culture will cease to reflect your values.

Most of these problems are avoidable if founders pay close attention to the culture within their company. The following are some of the red flags we've seen develop within teams.

You fail to recognize you've reached a new stage. Scrappiness is a great trait for startups to have early on. In the beginning, there are few resources, so you hack something together to find a way. This 'it's us against the world' attitude helps you hire and motivate the team. Staying scrappy can be the bedrock of a great culture because the attitude encourages innovation and resilience. But at some point, you have to stop seeing yourself as the little guy. It can be difficult to accept that what got you here isn't what will get you to the next stage. Your responsibilities grow. Your customers, suppliers, investors and teammates – perhaps your regulators – all have expectations about the kind of organization they're dealing with. You'll need to hire specialists and people who have scaled companies before. You may well need to be global and build teams of people with very different norms from the ones you started with. You can and should retain the elements of your culture that made you special, but culture needs to evolve to reflect your ambitions.

You describe your team as 'a family'. When your early-stage company is six people in a basement collaborating on an all-consuming project, it's natural to forge a bond. You see each other through hard times. You develop loyalty. You feel it's *more than a job*. But using familial language stops founders from having difficult conversations about what the company needs to succeed. You may end up with people in key positions that can't do what you need them to do, whose performance simply can't scale. Letting people go shouldn't mean you treat them callously, but starting from 'we're a family' makes it difficult to build the team you need without undermining morale.

A better metaphor is a 'top-tier sports team'. You can still build excellent rapport, but the right to a spot on the pitch is tied to performance, not emotional or unconditional loyalty.

You think you can fix it later. It can be easy to put off intentional culture building because you believe you'll have more time to sort it out later on. A good example of this is diversity. 'If your first five hires are white dudes, good luck getting a diverse team,' Sara Clemens said. 'That is going to be a hard problem you have to fix at 200 people because the white dudes are going to hire people they know and people like them. Whereas if you make the effort to hire five diverse people at the outset, you will bake in a diverse culture from the start.' Alan Mosca, co-founder at nPlan, a UK-based construction tech startup backed by Google Ventures, said, 'We made sure to create an attractive and inclusive culture for everyone, and that led to a healthy balance at the top of the funnel for most of our roles. This was our main metric. After that, we made sure to have a fair recruitment process that only looked at someone's ability to perform and grow within a role rather than biases on their background.'

You take on misaligned investors. Investors who don't share a founder's values create tension. The founder starts to behave as though they have a boss. The team detects a sudden change in the way the founder behaves and what the founder values. That can quickly alter the culture and create a real whiplash event for the team.

There's one EF company that's done a phenomenal job of refusing to let investors change their culture. They've been fortunate to gain exceptional traction, so they've been able to be selective. In their most recent round, they did a reverse pitch process – they asked investors to pitch them on how they could contribute to the company's mission. Even if you don't have that luxury, it's worth being clear and robust in communicating your company's culture to prospective investors.

You 'perform' culture instead of creating a culture of high performance. It is tempting to try to mirror the perks of major tech companies to lure talent: free food, massages on site, ping pong tables and the like. You might call this the cargo cult approach to culture, after the famous case of the Melanesian islanders in the South Pacific after WWII. During the war, the islanders experienced frequent airdrops of resources, first from the Japanese and then from the United States Air Force. Food and aid fell from the sky. After the war, it stopped happening. People on the island started building replica airstrips and mock control towers in hopes that the resources would return. (They did not.)

That might sound ridiculous, but it's amazing how many first-time founders look at Google and think something like, 'Wow, they nailed culture – it had free food and football tables and "20 per cent time" you could spend on other projects. If we do that, then we'll get Google-level performance.' Like the islanders, they're disappointed.

Google was able to introduce those benefits *because* it had great performance, not the other way around. Once you start to believe that what is special about your company is that it's fun, you forget that what super-talented people want above all is to do interesting, meaningful and challenging work.

You don't know when to sprint and when to run a marathon. Long working hours are a controversial topic in the startup community. There's certainly a risk of fetishizing late nights or weekend work for their own sake. No one wants a culture of 'presenteeism' or to ignore the toll that long hours place on relationships, family and sometimes even health. The reality, though, is that it's almost impossible to build an enormous company without very hard work. As Patrick Collison, co-founder of Stripe and investor in Entrepreneur First, has put it: 'While long hours can't be a goal… creating Stripe required obsessive intensity… long hours were needed for us to build something great.'[20]

The key is knowing how to balance this with sustainability. Startups take a long, long time to build. There are periods of extreme intensity

---

[20] Patrick Collison. 'While long hours can't be a goal, I worry that it's easy to mislead. As a descriptive matter, creating stripe required obsessive intensity. Maybe better founders could have worked "smarter", but I do know that long hours were needed for *us* to build something great.' Tweet. @patrickc (blog), June 4, 2019. https://twitter.com/patrickc/status/1135886195253284865.

and hard deadlines – and most of the time, venture-backed startups have a limited period of time to hit their traction goals or run out of money. But if you're going to do this for a decade, you probably can't sprint non-stop. Even the more determined entrepreneurs face burnout. As a founder, it's your job to set expectations and role model what you want to see in your team. To do this well, you need to know what it takes for you to stay healthy, balanced and happy. Great founders aren't afraid to talk openly about the trade-offs involved and signal clearly when the company needs to sprint and when to save energy for the marathon ahead.

One final note on culture. Culture is infrastructure for scale, but before you scale, you should be focused almost exclusively on your customer and iterating your idea. If you're a team of four people, and you're worried about your culture, something's gone wrong. Culture becomes more and more of a superpower the less and less you are directly involved in any given action in the company – and once you've got money in the bank and turn to hiring, it should be something you're building intentionally. But don't overthink it. Being a great place to work is a foundation that allows you to fulfil your mission, but you should never confuse it for your mission itself. Occasionally, we see strong cultures transform into navel-gazing ones. It's a non-obvious failure mode because usually it means that most people on the team *feel* great. But as soon as you lose focus on your customer's needs and building the product they want, you're in a dangerous place. You're trying to build a company, not a well-funded but short-lived cult. Put your customers at the heart of your culture and focus your efforts on them, and you'll eliminate most of your biggest problems.

Chapter Summary

You are responsible for building a company culture that stands in as a proxy for your presence.

- People notice what behaviours founders praise; focus on celebrating the behaviours you want to see and not the outcomes.
- Culture shouldn't be a performance; it should prioritize performance (i.e., culture is not about ping pong tables).
- Culture gains importance as the organization grows beyond the first few employees.

CHAPTER 16

What Happens Next?

Let's imagine you've raised your seed round and started hiring. The key elements for your startup are in place. You've identified your Edge and found a world-class co-founder with whom you've co-created a belief. Together, you've developed a hunch about an enormous problem. Through hours of listening to and learning from your customer, you've refined your idea. People are beginning to pay you to develop and deliver your product – you're starting to feel you might be close to product-market fit. You are a co-pilot on a plane taxiing the runway. But, alas, there is still no guarantee of a successful take-off.

First-time founders understandably make a lot of mistakes. In fact, so do second- and third-time founders. One of the most liberating aspects of startups is that for a sufficiently determined team working on a truly important problem, these mistakes are completely survivable. Advice abounds on overcoming the most obvious and debilitating mistakes (not spending enough time talking to customers, not launching soon enough, not managing cash properly and more). Even if you do find that you've made one of the classic mistakes, hopefully, one of your investors or advisors can help you navigate your way through.

Someone once said that raising venture capital was like a pie-eating contest where the prize is more pie. It's certainly true that while the problems change as your company grows, it rarely feels easier. In some ways, the biggest challenge is maintaining focus, determination and resilience through the long journey. It's important to be clear-eyed about what's coming. You can think of this as a continuation of the theme of psychological preparedness that we introduced at the start of the book. Perhaps the most alluring psychological mistake that founders make at this stage is something we call the step-change fallacy.

The Step-Change Fallacy

The step-change fallacy is the belief that there's one big thing that will permanently change the trajectory – even the fate – of your company. When you hear yourself saying something along the lines of 'If only X happened, it'd be a game-changer,' you are in a step-change fallacy mindset. The X can take a dizzying array of forms:

- If only we can get [insert respected influencer] to try our product…
- If only we can be featured on [insert widely consumed media outlet] …
- If only we can hire [insert big name] …
- If only we can raise money from [insert famous investor] …
- If only we can partner with [insert top-tier established brand] …

You are imagining that what comes after the ellipsis is a steep acceleration in performance, results or effectiveness. Aspirations like these are attractive because all the things you imagine in the square brackets do appear to be correlated with success. Great companies *do* get a lot of hot press and *do* raise funds from notable investors. As such, going after these results can look like an efficient shortcut.

In our experience, that's almost never true. You're flipping cause and effect. The glowing writeup in *WIRED*, the Series A from Sequoia – these are the *consequence* of unglamorous, dedicated hard work, not the cause. There is no single catalyst of a miraculous step change in your trajectory. There are no (repeatable) shortcuts in startups.

We have been guilty of the step-change fallacy at many points in our time building Entrepreneur First. What's striking is that when we *have* achieved milestones like these, we've seldom been going after them directly. And, looking back, we recognize how little they've mattered relative to the day-to-day work we do to improve our offering for entrepreneurs.

Preparation Meets Opportunity

The reason the step-change fallacy is so tempting is because successful startups go through transitions that look similar to step changes, at least from the outside. This is the 'overnight success' phenomenon: One moment a product seems niche, the next it's ubiquitous. (Discord is a great example of this in the last couple of years, but maybe the ultimate example is UiPath – it took 11 years from founding to Series A, but then just six years from Series A to $30bn IPO.)

Usually, though, what looks like blowing up overnight is actually an exponential growth curve becoming very steep. The distinction is important: a step change has the *appearance* of a miracle; a startup hitting the 'hockey stick' portion of the exponential growth curve is the sudden, explosive payoff from a long period of often unnoticed hard work.

It is a very poor strategy for a founder to bet on miracles. Moreover, even if 'miracles' happen, you can't make the most of them if you're not ready for them. A windfall opportunity can even be damaging. Suppose you did get Reid Hoffman's attention or hit the Reddit front page or were picked to pitch at TechCrunch Disrupt finals. Would you actually be in a position to take advantage of it? Or would you soon be drowning in retention problems, user confusion and complaints?

It's far better in the earliest stages to focus fully – and patiently – on understanding your customers and the problem you're solving. Invest in getting ready. Don't be tempted to chase after an illusory step-change moment.

'No shortcuts, no miracles,' as we like to say. It's less glamorous and harder work, but it's how great companies are built. And we hope this book is just the start of our relationship. Don't forget to go to howtobeafounder.com for resources. If you think we can help, get in touch.

Best of luck,

Matt and Alice

Bibliography

Startup mindset

The Start-up of You – Reid Hoffman and Ben Casnocha, Random House Business, 2013
Zero to One – Peter Thiel with Blake Masters, Virgin Books, 2015
Mindset – Dr Carol Dweck, Robinson, 2017
The Scout Mindset – Julia Galef, Piatkus, 2021

Co-founder relationships

Fierce Conversations – Susan Scott, Piatkus, 2017
Radical Candor – Kim Scott, Pan, 2019

Customer development

The Lean Startup – Eric Ries, Portfolio Penguin, 2011
The Mom Test – Rob Fitzpatrick, CreateSpace, 2013
The Startup Owner's Manual – Steve Blank, Wiley, 2020

Building your startup

Founders at Work – Jessica Livingston, Springer, 2011
The Hard Thing about Hard Things – Ben Horowitz, HarperBus, 2014
Super Founders – Ali Tamaseb, PublicAffairs, 2021
High Growth Handbook – Elad Gil, Stripe Press, 2018
Trillion Dollar Coach: The Leadership Playbook of Silicon Valley's Bill Campbell – Alan Eagle, Eric Schmidt and Jonathan Rosenberg, John Murray, 2020

Fundraising

Venture Deals – Brad Feld and Jason Mendelson, Wiley, 2019
Fundraising Field Guide – Carlos Eduardo Espinal, Reedsy, 2021

Go to www.howtobeafounder.com to find our full bibliography, including links to must-read articles and blogs.

Acknowledgements

First and foremost, we would like to thank the thousands of individuals who have joined Entrepreneur First. It's through working with you that we have been able to develop and hone the learnings we have shared in this book. It's been a privilege to work so closely with many of the world's most talented and ambitious individuals and to be a small part of their journey. Some have gone on to found some of the world's most important companies, and all have gone onto incredible careers making a significant impact in the world. We have learnt so much from all of you and continue to do so.

Second, there would be no book to write if it wasn't for the Entrepreneur First team who work with our aspiring entrepreneurs on a daily basis. Their hard work, diligence and dedication to being the team that founders want to work with has been instrumental in developing the learnings in this book. We're particularly grateful to the people who joined us before we had any evidence that EF would work and played such a key role in shaping the frameworks we discuss in the book.

Third, we have been lucky to work with some of the world's best investors over the last decade; without their faith and support, EF would not exist. We're especially grateful to our brilliant board members; Reid Hoffman, Charlie Songhurst, Alex Bangash, Toby Coppel, who have been so generous with their capital, time and networks.

How to Be a Founder would never have come together without the brilliant Sara Stibitz and Brianne Sanchez. It has been thought provoking and fun working with you, and we are so proud of what you've helped us produce. A big thank you to our team and alumni who provided feedback on early manuscripts and helped get the text to where it is now. And thank you to the team at Bloomsbury for being such supportive and encouraging publishers.

With full hearts, we would like to thank our coach Lucy Funnell, who worked with us from the very early days of Entrepreneur First. She sadly passed away recently, and we will forever be grateful for the support, challenge and good humour that she shared with us. We hope some of her wisdom is captured in these pages.

Finally, we couldn't have done this without our families. In particular, our spouses, Emily and Tom, who have been our rocks as we built Entrepreneur First. The life of a founder isn't always easy, and it's definitely not easy for those who have to live with them! Your love and support is foundational to what EF has become.

Index

accelerators   165, 166–8, 177
ADHD (attention deficit hyperactivity
      disorder)   21–2
advisors   188–9
ambition   1–3, 65–7
    and drive to achieve   20
    new kind of   2–3
Andreessen, Marc   69
angel investors   165, 168–9
annual recurring revenue (ARR)   176
applicability   15–16
attention deficit hyperactivity disorder
      (ADHD)   21–2
authenticity   67–8
    and judgement   55–6

B2B (business to business) products   147
B2C (business to consumer) products   147
backup plans   56–7
badge collecting   25–8
bank loans   163
barriers, breaking down   27–8, 33–4, 36–7
beliefs   128–31, 137, 154–5, 156
    founding beliefs   128–9
Bezos, Jeff   36
Bishop, Rob   131
board members   189–90
bootstrapping   162–3
Boussommier-Calleja, Alexandra   144
Branson, Richard   21
breakups   116–23, 130
    equity split   119–20, 121
    legal agreements   120–1
    no-stigma breakups   116–18
    vesting   121
Brin, Sergey   31
business to business (B2B) products   147
business to consumer (B2C) products   147
Butler, Pete   149–51

capital   30, 64–5, 66, 163, 165–6, 168: see also
      fundraising; venture capital
Carrell, Rachel   16
catalyst edge   80–3, 84
Chakraborty, Tuhin   122

Chan, Elixabeth   146–7
Chief Executive Officers (CEOs)   101–2,
      103, 120
    edges   102
    fundraising and   101–2
Chief Operating Officers (COOs)   103–4
Chief Technology Officers (CTOs)   103–4
Chiramel, Sachin   125
Clemens, Sara   142, 192, 198
co-founders
    breakups   47, 97–8, 116–23, 130
    choice of   97–110
    co-founder relationships x, 98, 130
    networks, current   106–8
    networks, potential   108–10
    number of co-founders required   99–100
    qualities   104–5
    roles   100–4
    testing   99, 112–15, 120, 125, 132, 136
    working with   112–23
coaches   187–8
Collison, Patrick   199
commerciality   15, 16
conflict   29, 101, 115, 116, 195
constraints: and creativity   126–7
COOs (Chief Operating Officers)   103–4
coronavirus pandemic   33
costs
    opportunity costs   4, 66, 91
    sunk costs   52
creativity: constraints and   126–7
credentialism   25–8
crowdfunding   173–4
CTOs (Chief Technology Officers)   103–4
culture   192–200
    behaviours   194–6
    building   193–6
    building, mistakes in   196–200
    conflict   195
    investors and   198
    long working hours   199–200
    and performance   198–9
    praise   194, 196
customer development   139–41, 145–8, 152
customer discovery   139–40, 141–5

daily debrief   114–15, 116
Dalyac, Alex   72–3, 85, 89
Davies, Christa   192
de Vries, Bas   13
deep learning   72–3, 89
dilution   171, 179–80
Dishpatch case study   149–51
diversity   198
Dixon, Chris   14, 134–5
Dorsey, Jack   14

edges   72–85, 87–96
    catalyst edge   80–3, 84
    CEOs and   102
    defining   83–5
    edge leverage   126–8
    finding   74–5, 91–2
    intersections   87–8, 90–1
    and learning   89–90, 94
    market edge   75–8, 83, 84
    maximizing success   89–91
    stack rank   85, 105
    strengthening ideas   89–90
    strengthening teams   90–1
    technical edge   78–80, 83, 84
    testing   91
    types of   75–83
    understanding   74
    using   87–96
Entrepreneur First viii–ix, x
    founding story   5–7
entrepreneurial ecosystems   38
entrepreneurship   1, 7
    technology entrepreneurship   3
equity
    advisor equity   188
    equity financing   163–4
    equity split   119–20, 121
exceptionalism   45
experience   77

failure   52
    backup plans   56–7
    causes of   43–50
    fear of   34–7
feedback   91–2, 116, 132, 146, 147
    daily debrief   114–15
finance   37–8
    money as cause of failure   44–5
    see also fundraising
First Round Capital   38
fit   73

founder-idea fit   73, 74, 89, 93
    product-market fit   89, 139
Fitzpatrick, Rob   140–2
fixed mindset   57, 58, 59
founder characteristics   11–23, 184
    articulating how ideas drive business   15–16
    challenging convention   16–18
    clarity of thought   14–15
    creating followership   20–1
    drive to achieve   19–20
    intellectual curiosity   13–14
    outliers   12–13
founder-idea fit   73, 74, 89, 93
founder mindset   51–9
founder stereotypes   34–7, 184
founding beliefs   128–9
Fuller, Buckminster   124
fundraising   90, 161–74, 175–82
    bootstrapping   162–3
    CEOs and   101–2
    equity financing   163–4
    investor choice   179–82
    scenario planning   176–7
    seed raise principles   177–9
    see also capital; venture capital

Gates, Bill   27
Ghadge, Pramod   76
Gil, Elad   100–1
Gorlin, Gena   51, 52, 54, 55
Graham, Paul   4–5, 99
growth mindset   12, 57–9, 80

Haco, Sasha   17
Heraclitus   1
Hewitt, Zoe Jervier   21
Hinrikus, Taavet   49
Hoffmann, Reid   32, 58, 77
hunches   128, 130–2, 143, 153–5
    refining   147
    sharing   145
    testing   131–2
Hussey-Yeo, Barney   78

idea maze   133–5
ideas   39–41
    strengthening   89–90
    testing   125, 136
ideation, linear   153–5
ideation framework   125, 126–33
    edges and   126–7
    phase 1: edge leverage   126–8

phase 2: beliefs   128–30
phase 3: hunches   130–2
phase 4: testing   132–3
in practice   135–6
implementation intentions   52–3
imposter syndrome   59
incubators   165
initial public offering (IPO)   169
innovation   127
intensity   49
internet   32–3
investments   165–73
investors   165–73
choosing   179–82
and culture   198
investor brand   181–2
relationships with   182
support from   180–1
terms   179–80
IPO (initial public offering)   169

Jobs, Steve   127
judgement   51–2
authenticity and   55–6

Kamprad, Ingvar   21

Landry, Tom   187–8
learning   17, 43–4, 58–9, 112–13, 114
deep learning   72–3, 89
edges and   89–90, 94
increased velocity of   89–90
traction and   112
legal agreements   120–1
letters of intent (LOIs)   144
Levie, Aaron   77
limited partners (LPs)   170
linear ideation   153–5
location   31–4
breaking down barriers   33–4
LOIs (letters of intent)   144
Lozano, Jesse   122–3
LPs (limited partners)   170

Mairs, Chris   102, 119–20, 189
market edge   75–8, 83, 84
market knowledge   76–7
market research   151–3
Maslow's hierarchy of needs   142
Mather, Toby   115, 136
meetings: daily debrief   114–15, 116
Meier, Maria   122

mentors   177, 185–6
mercenaries   67–8
mindsets
fixed mindset   57, 58, 59
founder mindset   51–9
growth mindset   12, 57–9, 80
minimum viable products (MVPs)   147, 148,
150, 151, 153
missionaries   67–8
mistakes, surviving   202–5
Molimpakis, Emilia   118
money: as cause of failure   44–5
Moodalagiri, Srinidhi   13, 87
Mosca, Alan   198
Murphy, Helen   76
MVPs (minimum viable products)   147, 148,
150, 151, 153
myths   124–5
breaking down barriers   27–8, 33–4, 36–7
credentialism   25–8
failure, fear of   34–7
founder stereotypes   37–9, 184
location   31–4
network size   28–31
perfectionism   39–41

networks   105–10, 143–4
current networks   106–8
network density   32
network size   28–31
potential networks   108–10
neurodiversity   21
no-stigma breakups   116–18

objectives and key results (OKRs)   viii–ix
objectivity   91
Obrecht, Cliff   19
Ologunebi, Andrew   17
opportunity: preparation and   204–5
opportunity costs   4, 66, 91
outliers   27

Page, Larry   31
partnerships   118–21
equity split   119–20, 121
legal agreements   120–1
vesting   121
Patel, Rayna   135–6
peer mentorship   186
Pelton, Alice   20–1
perfectionism   39–41
performance: and culture   198–9

Perkins, Melanie 19
personal exceptionalism 45
pivots 153–6
preparation: and opportunity 204–5
presenteeism 199
problems
    passion 94–5
    and solutions 90
procrastination 3–5
product-market fit 89, 139
productivity 112, 113
    testing 114

Qureshi, Zeena 144

racial bias 38–9
Ranca, Razvan 89
reality: and vision 54–5
regret 36–7
rejection 148
relationships 185
    with co-founders x, 98, 130
    with investors 182
    with mentors 185–6
right to win 92–5
    and want to win 94–5
risk 3–4, 34–6, 37
    reduction of 95–6
Roussel, Hervé Vũ 98
running into the spike 148–9
runway 177

SAFEs (Simple Agreement for Future
        Equity) 164 n. 17
Sandberg, Sheryl 185
scalability 64
    software companies 69–71
scale 63–5
scenario planning 176–7
self-honesty 51–4
sexism 38–9
Silbermann, Ben 18
Silicon Valley ix, 2–3, 31–4
Simple Agreement for Future Equity
        (SAFEs) 164 n. 17
software companies 173
    cost 70
    economics 70
    reach 69
    scalability 69–71
    scope 69–70
Spenner, Leo 130

spike: running into the spike 148–9
Srinivasan, Balaji 133
stack ranking 28
    edges and 85, 106
startup ecosystems 32, 33–4
startup ideas 39–41
step-change fallacy 203–4
Stokes, Patrica 126–7
success: maximization of 89–91
sunk costs 52
surveys 141

Tahi, Yassine 145
talent 66
talent investors 165, 166–8
Tamaseb, Ali 64, 67
team-building 90–1
technical edge 78–80, 83, 84
technology entrepreneurship 3
tenacity 49
testing 40–1, 57, 99, 131–3
    edges 91
    hunches 131–2
    ideas 125, 136
    productivity 114
    team testing 99, 112–15, 120, 125, 132, 136
Thiel, Peter 30, 137
Thomson, Alistair 17
time: as cause of failure 45–6
timelines 136–7
traction 45, 47, 112
    learning and 112

validation 28
vanity metrics 64–5
venture capital 12, 30, 32–3, 169–73
venture capitalists (VCs) 165, 168
    business model 66
    support from 180–1
vesting 121
vision: and reality 54–5
Voltaire (François-Marie Arouet) 24

want to win 94–5
Wiklund, Johan 21–2
willingness 100–2
willpower: and failure 45, 46–50
Wolfe Herd, Whitney 75–6

Young, Erica 107–8

Zennström, Niklas 129–30
Zuckerberg, Mark 27, 30